PRAISE FOR *FORMULA 2+2*

"If you think managing and evaluating employees is frustrating, time-consuming, and exhausting, then read this book—right now! You will find out how to help employees be more productive, and you'll help them to learn at a faster rate. And your own job might become more satisfying in the process. While you're at it, buy a copy for your boss."

   —**Dorothy Marcic, Vanderbilt University,**
      author of *Managing with the Wisdom of Love*

"The most practical book I have read since *One Minute Manager*. On a single plane flight I learned a system that I can begin using tomorrow. This book should become a standard reference for those searching for a better way of managing and coaching."

   —**James M. Theroux, Flavin Professor of Management,**
      Isenberg School of Management, University of Massachusetts

"In *Formula 2+2*, Doug and Dwight Allen have taken a not-so-simple cybernetic concept and transformed it into an effective, memorable, actionable process. That's no small accomplishment and managers, their organizations, and their employees are the beneficiaries. Here's a book as useful to CEOs as it is to first-line supervisors."

   —**Jim Griesemer, Dean, Daniels College of Business,**
      University of Denver

"*Formula 2+2* addresses one of the most difficult human resource management challenges facing Chinese managers: giving effective performance feedback to employees without causing a loss of face. This balanced approach encourages direct feedback with a constructive spirit."

   —**Xu Erming, Dean, School of Business,**
      Renmin University of China, Beijing

"Formula 2+2 adds a powerful tool to the construction managers' 'toolbox' as they seek ways to coach their employees and hold them accountable for doing a great job."

—**Chuck Shinn, President of Lee Evans Group Management Seminars for Homebuilders**

"At Starbucks we learned that providing regular feedback through the 2+2 system was far more effective than traditional performance review cycles."

—**Kerry Plemmons, Former Regional Manager, Starbucks**

Formula
2+2

THE KEN BLANCHARD SERIES
SIMPLE TRUTHS UPLIFTING THE VALUE OF PEOPLE
IN ORGANIZATIONS

The Referral of a Lifetime
The Networking System That Produces
Bottom-Line Results . . . Every Day!
Tim Templeton

The Serving Leader
5 Powerful Actions That Will Transform Your Team,
Your Business, and Your Community
Ken Jennings and John Stahl-Wert

Your Leadership Legacy
The Difference You Make in People's Lives
Marta Brooks, Julie Start,
and Sarah Caverhill

Formula 2+2
The Simple Solution for Successful Coaching
Douglas B. Allen and Dwight W. Allen

Formula
2+2

The Simple Solution for
Successful Coaching

Douglas B. Allen
Dwight W. Allen

BK

BERRETT-KOEHLER PUBLISHERS, INC.
San Francisco

Berrett-Koehler Publishers, Inc.
235 Montgomery Street, Suite 650
San Francisco, CA 94104-2916
Tel: (415) 288-0260   Fax: (415) 362-2512   www.bkconnection.com

Ordering Information
Quantity sales. Special discounts are available on quantity purchases by corporations,
associations, and others. For details, contact the "Special Sales Department" at the
Berrett-Koehler address above.
Individual sales. Berrett-Koehler publications are available through most bookstores.
They can also be ordered direct from Berrett-Koehler: Tel: (800) 929-2929;
Fax: (802) 864-7626; www.bkconnection.com.
Orders for college textbook/course adoption use. Please contact Berrett-Koehler:
Tel: (800) 929-2929; Fax: (802) 864-7626.
Orders by U.S. trade bookstores and wholesalers. Please contact Publishers Group
West, 1700 Fourth Street, Berkeley, CA 94710. Tel: (510) 528-1444; Fax (510) 528-3444.

Berrett-Koehler and the BK logo are registered trademarks
of Berrett-Koehler Publishers, Inc.

Printed in the United States of America

Berrett-Koehler books are printed on long-lasting acid-free paper. When it is available,
we choose paper that has been manufactured by environmentally responsible processes.
These may include using trees grown in sustainable forests, incorporating recycled
paper, minimizing chlorine in bleaching, or recycling the energy produced at the
paper mill.

Library of Congress Cataloging-in-Publication Data

Allen, Douglas B., 1955-
  Formula 2+2 : the simple solution for successful coaching /
Douglas B. Allen and Dwight W. Allen.
    p. cm.
  ISBN 1-57675-310-7
    1. Supervision of employees. 2. Employees—Counseling of.
3. Employees—Rating of. 4. Employee motivation. 5. Mentoring in
business. 6. Feedback (Psychology) I. Title: Formula two plus two.
II. Title: Successful coaching. III. Allen, Dwight William. IV. Title.

HF5549.12.A528 2005
658.3'124—dc22   2004050272

First Edition
09 08 07 06 05 04   10 9 8 7 6 5 4 3 2 1

Copyediting and proofreading by PeopleSpeak.
Book design and composition by Beverly Butterfield, Girl of the West Productions.

To our families!

CONTENTS

I am thrilled to have Dwight and Doug Allen's book, *Formula 2+2: The Simple Solution for Successful Coaching,* as part of my Berrett-Koehler series. The authors are two of the brightest people I have ever met, and they're bringing new insights and creativity to an area that badly needs help: performance feedback.

So often when I ask people, "How do you know whether you're doing a good job?" they tell me, "I haven't been chewed out lately by my boss." In other words, no news is good news. Too many managers are "seagull" managers. They're not around until there's something wrong; then they fly in, make a lot of noise, dump on everybody, and fly out. All too often, feedback from managers focuses on the negative.

In this marvelous book, Doug and Dwight Allen rightfully contend that many people think performance feedback is "about as much fun as a trip to the dentist." They suggest there is a better way. Their 2+2 system is an ongoing coaching and feedback process that can supplement and humanize feedback strategy and make it more effective for any manager.

With the 2+2 process, when managers or leaders meet with a member of their team, they share at least two compliments—two positive behaviors they've noticed the person doing that deserve to be recognized. This is a formula for success because when people feel appreciated, they drop their defenses and become willing to listen to feedback. Then the manager or leader makes two suggestions—ideas that might help the person improve. As a result of this process, there is a wonderful balance in the kind of feedback people receive.

Dwight Allen has been a seminal thinker in human development for many years. I first met him in the late 1960s at Ohio University in Athens, Ohio, where I went—straight out of graduate school at Cornell University—for my first teaching opportunity. Dwight was on campus to give a public lecture to people interested in education. After he was introduced, he pulled a hundred-dollar bill out of his pocket, held it up, and said, "I'll give this hundred-dollar bill to anyone in this audience who can name for me the capitals of North and South Dakota and North and South Carolina."

No one in the audience could name all the capitals. Dwight laughed and said, "How many of you had to take a capitals test when you were in school?" A knowing smile came across everyone's face. Then Dwight said, "I once caught a teacher giving a capitals test to her class. When I asked why she didn't put atlases around the room during the test so the kids could look up the answers, she said, 'I can't do that; all the kids would get them right.'"

Dwight laughed again and said, "What is education? A zero-sum game? Some win and some lose? Somebody once asked Einstein what his telephone number was and he went to a phone book. An intelligent person knows how to find information, not store it."

With that introduction, Dwight completely captured my imagination. I had always felt that performance evaluation was a problem in organizations. Most of the focus was put on sorting people out and making sure that not too many people won. That really bothered me. Dwight's thinking unleashed all kinds of options when it came to managing people's performance.

By the time Dwight concluded his lecture with his big-picture dream and vision for education, he had me hooked. It wasn't even a year later that Margie and I followed him to Amherst, Massachusetts, where Dwight had taken over as dean of the School of Education. We wanted to "chase his windmill." Dwight felt we could get better results in education by random chance than by doing what we were doing. He eliminated all the courses that were being taught and we started over from scratch. When I arrived, I taught Experimental Classes 155, 156, and 157. As I look back, those years were the most exciting I have ever had in education.

During my years at Amherst I also met Doug Allen. I was delighted to reconnect with him a few years ago. As you'll see in these pages, Doug is as creative a thinker as his dad.

Read this book. Practice the concepts presented. I guarantee it will make a difference in the way your organization operates. The 2+2 feedback and coaching system will help you develop enthusiastic people to better serve your customers and contribute greatness to your organization.

KEN BLANCHARD
COAUTHOR OF *THE ONE MINUTE MANAGER*®

INTRODUCTION BY BILL COSBY

Though I've never really thought about it before, *Formula 2+2* has led me to realize that I've depended upon feedback and encouragement all my life. I know that if people ever stop laughing, I'm in trouble. Take my concert performances for instance. The live audience is all about feedback. The spontaneous laughs, applause—even the occasional jeer—all tell me whether I'm on track and getting my message across.

The real-time feedback I rely upon is frequently missing from the workplace. In many organizations, the only feedback you can count on is the annual evaluation, and it is almost always stale news by the time you get it. "Speedy" feedback is defined as semiannual or quarterly appraisal—not much better. Too often, the little feedback offered is feared, not welcomed.

In comedy it's the other way around. It's the immediate and positive feedback that keeps you going. When the laughter stops, you know you have to do something different—and fast. Comedy involves lots of improvisation. Even tried-and-true routines are adapted to the audience in real time—you need to respond to the moment. Isn't it obvious that the workplace should encourage a similar response to the moment? But that's pretty unrealistic if immediate response means as soon as possible—after the semiannual review!

That's why this book is so important. If you take it to heart, its message can change your whole attitude toward feedback. I have seen firsthand how this can happen. At the University of Massachusetts, where I was a doctoral student, Dwight Allen created a school of education that lived and breathed feedback and encouragement. The results were amazing, and that same spirit is captured in this book.

Dwight and his son Doug have woven a fine story, telling of the current woes and bright hopes for feedback and encouragement. If you follow their lead, you will be able to engage in great feedback conversations—with your employees, your colleagues, even your family!

The 2+2 concept sounds simple: a balance of compliments and suggestions given on a regular basis. It is simple, but not that simple. The trick is in the delivery. When I was a kid, we knew that when Grandma gave us "the look," the feedback we were getting was anything but balanced. All too frequently, feedback in the workplace sure feels like "the look."

Formula 2+2 can help you replace "the look" with a balance of compliments and suggestions. If my audiences just sat there, satisfied but not laughing (or even worse, giving me "the look"), I would soon be looking for new material—or a new audience. Receiving compliments can help prepare us to hear the more difficult things. It makes us comfortable about what we are doing right—and eager to do more. Suggestions provide us with the opportunity to improve—en route to receiving even more compliments.

You'll like what Doug and Dwight say; and I like the way they say it. The next time you are tempted to give someone "the look," try using 2+2!

BILL COSBY, ED.D.

PROLOGUE

Luna 1 was launched and away on its unprecedented journey through space. It was January 2, 1959, and there was a high level of excitement at the remote launch site in the USSR. Scientists were attempting what no one had ever tried before: to hit the moon with a rocket launched from Earth.

It missed.

Ten years later, there was equal excitement in the mission control center of *Apollo 11*. This time the result was quite different. "Hitting" the moon had become so routine that it was not even an issue—the excitement was in the expectation that Neil Armstrong and Buzz Aldrin would actually walk on the moon for the first time in history. We were not disappointed.

Much had changed in ten years. Perhaps most important was the fact that we had learned how to make in-flight corrections—guidance coupled with feedback. Scientists could launch a rocket in the general direction of the moon with complete confidence that the rocket could be "steered" to reach the moon—or even more remote celestial targets millions of miles away.

Our space team had learned that constant performance appraisal and feedback were required in the effective guidance of a rocket. But somehow most managers have not learned that we must make this same level of confident correction in our dealings with people.

The principle is simple and obvious, not only in rocket science but also in everyday life. We would not think of driving a car without midcourse corrections. When it veers even slightly to the left or right, an immediate small touch on the steering wheel restores the proper direction. But when an employee is "launched" into a complex task or series of tasks, often feedback is either missing entirely, given too late, or offered in an inappropriate way.

> Regular feedback helps keep rockets— and people— on target.

We can do better. The results can be as awesome as routinely hitting the moon. We want to tell you how a simple feedback process called 2+2 can be used to improve the way we work with one another so that we can hit our own management targets. Armed with the correct attitudes and tools, our potential for success will be realized because feedback can be given and received at every level. In an increasingly complex, rapidly changing workplace, we are constantly exploring unknowns in tasks and relationships. Feedback is the only means for staying on target. Join us in exploring a new concept of mission control in the business environment!

ONE

The Unguided Missile

Percy Pershing was out of control again. His supervisor, Pauline Smith, was frustrated—and the company was hurting.

Pauline prided herself in running a tight ship. She supervised twenty salespeople, encouraging them to sell and service energetically the firm's high-quality products. Customer feedback on the product line continued to be extremely positive. However, sales had been relatively flat for the past two years and the company just couldn't seem to capitalize on its product excellence in the marketplace.

Percy's recent trends were a case in point. As she looked at the latest sales report, Pauline saw two lines on a graph. One line, which represented the sales goals she and Percy had agreed upon six months previously, headed toward the northeast corner of the chart. The other line—actual sales for the reporting period—dipped and dived erratically on its downward path toward the southeast corner of the graph. *Percy is as unpredictable as an unguided missile,* Pauline thought.

This report was only the latest of several that had delivered equally bad news regarding Percy's performance over the past several months. Pauline liked Percy and did not look forward to the prospect of confronting him. Until six months ago, Percy had been one of her best salespeople, and she did not want to

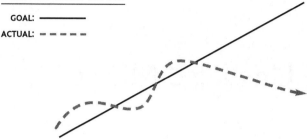

discourage him. She had hoped that by giving him some time and encouragement, he might self-correct and the problem would go away. She knew that Percy meant well, and she had originally decided to wait until the formal performance appraisal at the end of the year to raise her concerns with him.

But this latest report was the straw that broke the camel's back. Percy's sales hadn't improved. In fact, they had declined further. She decided that as much as she hated the prospect, she would need to have a serious talk with him. She called him and scheduled a meeting for the next day.

In this brief meeting, she tried to remain friendly and supportive as she delivered the bad news. "If sales do not improve, you won't receive your year-end bonus."

She had given him ample time to change his course. She had cut him as much slack as any reasonable manager could. He was now facing his last chance.

+++

Of course, Percy had a different view of the situation. In the intervening months since his last performance appraisal, Percy had assumed that no news was good news. He knew that he wasn't even close to achieving his goals—for the second quarter in a row—but he was also aware that other people were experiencing similar problems. It's not that he wasn't trying. He had put in more than his fair share of hours and had done his best to provide good service to his customers. Surely Pauline could see that. He had expected at least some positive comments from her.

Instead, Percy left Pauline's office feeling shocked and betrayed. She had been cordial enough, but instead of acknowledging his hard work, she had focused on the poor sales. Didn't she realize he was doing his best? Didn't she realize how much extra time he had been putting in? Even when he hadn't met his sales quotas, he had spent a lot of extra time with customers after the sale to help them install the product and learn how to use it.

Pauline is as unpredictable as an unguided missile, Percy thought. As he looked toward the future, he concluded that it would be increasingly difficult to work in an environment where the capricious and unpredictable behavior of his manager placed his compensation—and perhaps even his job security—at risk.

+++

In contrast to Percy's feelings of betrayal, Pauline was simply confused. Percy had actually seemed surprised when she told him in a very calm, friendly way that his work was not satisfactory. After all, they had mutually agreed on clear goals that had not been met. In reality, he had not even come close. How could he have been surprised?

As unpleasant as the meeting had become, she still hoped Percy could turn himself around. It would take considerable time and money to find another employee to replace him. By the time the new person was up to speed, another year of vital new account sales development would be lost.

Pauline was confident that she was a good manager. She had high expectations for her team. She set challenging goals for herself and for her people. She encouraged them to come to her with problems and offered them her support in numerous ways.

She believed in empowerment, too. She let her salespeople take initiative and encouraged them to work directly with anyone within the organization to solve problems and respond more effectively to customers. She was the kind of manager she wished she'd had when she was a sales rep years ago.

As she reflected on her encounter with Percy, she determined that she would have to reinforce the company's goals as clearly as possible during his performance appraisal at the end of the year.

+++

Pauline just doesn't know how to manage, Percy thought. *I do my best, but my best is not good enough for a manager who doesn't know what she wants from her people.*

Had this been an isolated incident, Percy might have simply dismissed it as the result of Pauline's grumpiness on a bad day. Most managers have those every once in a while—as do most people. But he had heard from too many of his colleagues about similar incidents. As a result, the company had lost many valuable and talented people.

Just two months earlier, Mandy had complained bitterly to Percy about a run-in she had had with Pauline. Her sales figures had shown improvement over the preceding months, yet Pauline had called her and had spoken sharply about an isolated complaint she had received from one of Mandy's customers. While Pauline had made a valid point about the problem with that customer, she hadn't made any mention of the hundreds of satisfied customers Mandy had worked with over the past several years. In fact, Mandy had become so de-motivated by Pauline's phone call that she abandoned a new system she had developed called "personal selling excellence," or PSE. Her sales—and her enthusiasm—continued to decline until one day she was gone. Percy had no idea where she went.

Meanwhile, Sena, another of Percy's counterparts, always seemed to be spinning his wheels. He was capable and motivated but had never been in a sales position before. He worked hard and was enthusiastic but didn't know the first thing about selling the company's products. Percy could see that Sena's job would be in jeopardy if someone didn't offer him some friendly advice on basic selling techniques. Percy had considered talking to Sena himself. Here was a real tragedy in the making—a potentially great salesperson was failing because he didn't know he was going about his job in an entirely ineffective manner. Percy decided it really wasn't his business and he didn't want to intrude. A few days later, Sena was gone.

> Great employees may fail without adequate feedback.

Finally there was Greg, the top salesperson in the organization. Percy didn't know where Greg ended up when he left the company, but he did know that Greg's departure, too, had been entirely unnecessary. When the company had downsized its sales force about two years earlier, the sales force was shocked to see two of the hardest-working salespeople get pink slips. While it was widely known that two other salespeople, Carrie and Yvette, had missed their sales quotas and were generally lazy when it came to helping their colleagues and customers, they had remained in the company unscathed while two spirited performers had been asked to leave. Greg had watched this process carefully and wondered if he could be next. This led to so much insecurity on his part that he decided to move on.

Pauline was taken entirely by surprise on that one and expressed her regret that the top salesperson in her organization was leaving. She even offered him a bonus to encourage him to reconsider, but he left nonetheless.

Percy recalled that when the layoffs hit, Greg had confided in him. He had said that he had no confidence in the integrity of the company's feedback and reward system. He knew he was excellent at what he did and would have no trouble finding another great job. As much as he liked the company, he felt that in the event of another downsizing, his job would be as much at risk as anyone's. He wasn't sure how much he was valued, and he didn't see any connection between who performed and who was ultimately laid off.

As Percy reflected on some of these recent incidents, he again wondered whether he should look for another job himself.

✦✦✦

As puzzling as Percy's response had been to their conversation earlier in the day, Pauline had to admit that it wasn't the first time she had been caught by surprise by one of her people's reaction to the feedback she had provided. She believed she was skilled at guiding them. She worked with them each year to set challenging yet attainable goals. She tried to avoid giving negative feedback, but if matters got too bad, she would meet with individuals privately so they wouldn't be embarrassed. She also held regular meetings with her staff to benchmark and discuss organization progress. And as much as she hated the process, she spent an inordinate amount of time preparing for and conducting the company's formal performance appraisals at the end of each year. What else could she reasonably do to communicate her position to people when matters were not going well?

Admittedly, Pauline loathed the whole idea of performance appraisals—nasty pieces of paper that had to be filled out in great detail. Even so, she had considered changing from annual reviews to semiannual reviews. She thought perhaps this would help keep her team on track. After all, the annual approach didn't seem to accomplish anything meaningful.

On her commute home, Pauline decided that there had to be a better way to give her employees feedback. And she was determined to find it.

KEY TAKEAWAYS

- Inadequate and inconsistent feedback leads to frustrated people and managers alike.

- Without a proper context, even well-intentioned feedback can result in shock and defensiveness.

- The formal performance appraisal system is usually not an effective vehicle for providing regular feedback to people.

TWO

Performance Appraisal:
Like a Trip to the Dentist

Pauline had trouble falling asleep that night. She kept tossing and turning as her thoughts about performance appraisals churned around in her head.

Might as well get up and make some notes, she thought as she threw the bed covers aside.

She turned on the light in her home office and booted up her laptop. The first words she entered were "Annual PAs: About as much fun as a trip to the dentist."

This could help both me and the company, she thought as she began to collect and enter her ideas. It was clear to her that there were several reasons for her disdain of annual performance appraisals.

First, they were time consuming. Pauline resented all the time she spent filling out forms. Each form asked for a lot of repetitive information that she had to copy laboriously from the previous year's form, followed by forty performance items she had to evaluate.

The meetings themselves were time consuming, too. She had to sit down with each employee for a half hour, an hour, or more and talk with him or her. The meetings seemed to go on forever and often ended on a sour note, even though that was never her intention. It somehow just "happened."

Second, she was concerned about the use of arbitrary numbers. Each section involved rating her people on a one to five scale. It was very difficult to justify giving one person a four and another a five. What was the behavioral difference between a four and a five? How could she be impartial and objective using numbers? While she could distinguish between the best and worst of her people, most were in the mushy middle. So she tended to give all of her folks high numbers because she didn't want to prevent any of them from getting their full—if rather meager—bonuses at the end of the year.

Another problem was that performance appraisals usually involved coordination with the human resources department. These people, after all, were the custodians of the performance appraisal process. They were cordial and helpful enough, but HR didn't understand the day-to-day realities of line managers. They wanted the forms back by a certain date regardless of the work pressures Pauline confronted. It was as if those blasted pieces of paper were more important than the customers in the field. Pauline was incensed that a department to which she did not report was ordering her to do something arbitrary at best—and totally at its convenience.

It was clear to Pauline that her direct supervisor, Andy, viewed performance appraisals as a low priority. After all, he seldom completed his appraisals within the two-month time frame set by the HR department. In fact, Pauline had never received her own performance appraisal anywhere near the deadline. And when she met with Andy to discuss her appraisal, she learned very little because, clearly, he hadn't taken the time to prepare for the meeting.

Due to his low opinion of the process, she received little support in terms of the reviews she conducted. In all of the years she had worked with Andy, he had not once raised the issue of how well she was appraising her people's performance. Certainly it was not something evaluated or even mentioned in his appraisal of her performance.

Pauline wondered how Andy would respond if she said, "Sorry, I can't meet your production quota this week because I'm taking the time to do effective and timely performance appraisals with my staff."

His response would be as predictable as the weather in Portland, she thought. "Have you lost your mind? You can fill out those appraisal papers anytime. We have customer orders to fill." It turned out that there were always customer orders to fill, so performance appraisals routinely slipped to the bottom of the priority list. When most managers finally got around to preparing appraisals, they didn't devote the time and attention needed to do them well because HR needed them yesterday.

The forms were also devilishly annoying to fill out because they required subjective as well as objective analysis. As hard as the numbers were to assign, at least they were numbers. Pauline could then use those numbers to justify her discussion with an employee:

Performance appraisals often read like ancient history.

"Right now you are a three; perhaps you can work harder this year and move to a four." But the form also had space to write a qualitative assessment of the employee.

Pauline was especially uncomfortable with this aspect. She believed that a manager's job was to be objective. Any narrative she wrote about one of her people's performance ran the risk of subjectivity and bias. If she prided herself on anything, it was her fairness and unbiased approach toward all of her people. It occurred to her that perhaps the performance appraisal system could be improved by redesigning the forms to eliminate the request for subjective assessments.

The fact that performance appraisals took place only once a year was a big problem. By the time Pauline completed the forms and shared them with her employees, much of the content was ancient history.

But to Pauline, one of the most frustrating aspects of the current performance appraisal process was that it did not have a clearly established purpose in Pauline's company. How were those numbers and subjective statements actually used? Pauline knew that they impacted bonuses and that was why she tended to rate everyone positively. After all, she didn't have any really *bad* people. Even the poorest performer among them deserved more than the meager bonus offered by the company. While she couldn't change the amount of the bonuses, she could at least make sure that all of her people got as much money as possible.

Even her best people had occasional bad months. Yet when that did happen, she generally did not reflect that fact in their performance appraisals. She was afraid that this might stigmatize the work records of her people and limit their consideration for future promotions. From a selfish standpoint, of course, Pauline liked to do what she could to retain her best people. But Pauline genuinely cared about the career development of her staff and wanted to help them get ahead in the company. By overlooking her people's occasional poor performances, Pauline believed she was serving their best interests in the long run.

Of course, the number one problem with performance appraisals was that they often involved the delivery of bad news.

> Performance appraisals may be feared as bearers of bad news.

Even though she rated most people high, she still felt obliged to raise concerns with her people during a performance appraisal meeting. This was the one structured opportunity she had in which to do this. She used the occasion to broach issues that had not been discussed during the year. Because both she and her people knew that this was going to happen, the meetings usually got off to an uncomfortable start and remained uncomfortable throughout.

Pauline looked at the list she had entered in her computer—a list she felt summarized the problem with performance appraisals fairly well.

Okay, Pauline thought. *Now that I know what I don't like about appraisals, who's going to care?*

With that, Pauline put her computer to "sleep" and pushed her unpleasant thoughts about performance appraisals to the back of her mind. She never bothered to print out her thoughts. In fact, she simply forgot about them.

KEY TAKEAWAYS

- PAs are time consuming.

- They use arbitrary numbers.

- HR doesn't understand what pressures managers face.

- PAs are a low priority to management.

- Management offers little support for the process.

- PAs are subjective as well as objective.

- They contain ancient history.

- They have no clearly established purpose.

- They might stigmatize work records.

- They deliver bad news.

THREE

The Trip to the Dentist

Three months later, Pauline was in an unusually foul mood. She had never presented her thoughts on performance appraisals to her boss nor to anyone in HR, so, naturally, nothing had changed.

Worse yet, she was already two weeks overdue in preparing Percy's evaluation. She had deliberately left his for last—an avoidance tactic, for certain. Fortunately, Percy's sales performance had picked up nicely since their somewhat unpleasant conversation, so she didn't really have anything important to say to him. But the annual appraisal had to be done—whether she liked it or not—and she knew it would be a stressful experience, no matter what.

"Might as well get on with it," she said to herself aloud. "Hmm, let's see. Quantity of Work? Good. Quality of Work? Good. Aha, here's one! Relations with Peers?"

Pauline remembered that Percy had engaged in a harsh exchange with Lindsay, a new rep who had given an incorrect quote to one of Percy's customers eight months ago. Pauline decided to mention that incident and rated Percy as "needs improvement" on his relations with peers. When it came to "supports company objectives," Pauline knew that Percy had been letting sales slide with the larger industrial customers, even though it had been agreed in a staff meeting in which Percy was present that the larger customers should receive more attention. Another item that "needs improvement."

It was difficult to find reasonable comments to make for so many of the items. What could she say about "timeliness"? Percy was usually on time but occasionally showed up late for staff meetings when he had been with clients. Should she mention that? *Oh well, might as well remind him that he's been late a few times.*

> It's difficult to find reasonable comments to make for so many items.

Pauline gave Percy top ratings for productivity—no question about that. He had been among her top salespeople for three years in a row notwithstanding that six-month slump she had discussed with him several weeks ago. But as far as "creativity" was concerned, he hadn't really suggested anything new this year. Of course, last year he had helped her completely revise the way the department kept track of client needs and had developed a tickler system to remind clients when it was time to reorder, so she marked his creativity as "average." Average is safe when you don't have anything in particular to say.

She completed her "general comments" by saying that she was sure Percy "will do better next year." Pauline knew that Percy was an old hand at this. He was aware that these personnel appraisal routines didn't mean much anyway.

✛ ✛ ✛

Pauline phoned Percy and asked if she could stop by to give him his performance appraisal. She hadn't visited him on his turf for several months, but that was fine with him, as he didn't mind being left alone. Although he'd been frustrated by the meeting they'd had several months earlier, that was water under the bridge. He knew he was the top performer in the division, so he wasn't concerned about the appraisal.

Percy looked up as Pauline came into his office. She handed him the appraisal and said, "It's time for performance evaluations." She turned abruptly and left his office without further comment.

Percy was more than a little curious as he opened the envelope. *Wonder why she just dropped it in my lap and left.* As he read the appraisal, his curiosity turned to anger.

For starters, Percy was irritated that Pauline mentioned the incident involving Lindsay, the new rep who had lost a big sale by misquoting prices. Percy knew he might have handled the conflict better, but Lindsay had cost him almost a thousand bucks in commissions. Since then, however, he and Lindsay had developed a great working relationship. He had shown Lindsay the ropes—Lindsay was an eager learner—and Lindsay had helped him close an even bigger sale than the one he had botched. *Pauline is really out to lunch. She doesn't have a clue about what is going on, and she's accusing me of needing improvement in working with people,* he thought bitterly.

In Percy's opinion, the rest of the appraisal was garbage, too. The comments about working with large customers were ridiculous. His company simply wasn't competitive, and he found that he could spend his time much more productively with smaller customers. After all, that's what the sales task is all about—the bottom line. And his bottom line was better than anybody's, though no one would ever know it by reading Pauline's performance appraisal.

If only this company were a bit more flexible on its discount schedule for our large industrial customers, there would be lots of potential with those companies. But no one is ever interested in listening to me. I've known that all along, and this stupid appraisal just proves it!

He was particularly burned by the rating of "average" for creativity. Last year he had helped design a new system that saved megabucks for the company and helped all the reps work their contact lists more efficiently. He didn't make a nickel on that suggestion, but those were the days when he had felt more appreciated. Pauline was newer then. She was easier to work with and not so arrogant. He had lots of suggestions then—and could offer even more now. Unfortunately, Pauline had changed and it wasn't even worth bringing up his ideas to her. She simply was not interested in listening.

At least Pauline got one right when she gave him the top mark for productivity. Even she wasn't so blind that she couldn't read recent sales numbers. He had been number one for the past two months.

When Percy got to the last comment—"I'm sure Percy will do better next year"—a sly little smile broke out on his face. Last week he had been called by the company's chief competitor and had been offered a job that would pay about the same to start. However, if everything worked out, in six months he would be promoted to manager and receive a 50 percent raise. At the time, he hadn't been that interested because it would require him to move his family to another city. But this disgusting performance appraisal made the decision for him.

He signed the performance appraisal—another stupid part of the process—as if he had any choice or even had the opportunity to indicate on the form what was really going on. Then he put on his coat and, with the appraisal in hand, he went to Pauline's office. He marched past her secretary without a word, burst in on Pauline, and threw the appraisal on her desk.

Pauline looked up in shock. Without missing a beat, Percy thundered, "I'm tired of your criticism and random complaining! I'm outta here! I quit! You'll have my formal letter in the morning. And I wouldn't be surprised if half the department quits with me."

Percy didn't even go back to his office. He went down to his car and drove home to call his new boss.

+++

Pauline was stunned. She couldn't see what had set Percy off. She had given him pretty good ratings. He knew he was tops. This stupid appraisal procedure just made the situation more difficult. The entire company would be better off if it ditched the entire process. She knew, too, that there would be major fallout from the fact that Percy had quit.

In tears and at her wit's end, Pauline called her longtime friend and mentor, Audrey. Audrey was a well-respected educator in the field of performance management whom Pauline had met in a seminar five years before.

"Great to hear from you," said Audrey. "What's new?"

Pauline described the situation—how she was required by HR to conduct annual performance evaluations and how her latest round of appraisals had backfired on her in a big way. She explained that she had lost several top performers during recent months, Percy being the latest of the defectors. She confessed her concern that other people would follow in Percy's steps and jump ship.

"You gave me great insights in your seminar, and I've studied your materials again and again since then. I've tried to carry your guidelines over into our annual performance appraisals. Now this happens! What have I been doing wrong?"

"It's not that you're doing anything wrong," Audrey suggested. "The concepts that I presented in my seminars were right for the times. But times have changed. Business has changed. And HR departments and line managers have to team up to work together in the new world."

"I don't understand," Pauline confessed. "We're still in essentially the same business. Our products have been updated, our solutions have changed, but we're still selling the same basic goods and services."

"That's exactly my point. Even though businesses offer the same basic services, the way of doing business has changed. Needs have progressed. Channels, thanks to developments such as the Internet and enterprise software, are being transformed in real time. Solutions have had to keep pace with rapid change. Speed is a requirement for organizational success."

Pauline protested. "What does all this have to do with annual performance evaluations?"

"You just said the key word: 'annual.' Businesses today can't keep up to speed if they rely upon annual or even quarterly cycles for their business processes. The pace of business has changed. In order to achieve spirited performance from the members of your team, you have to find a way to provide *constant* feedback and coaching."

"Constant?" Pauline was incredulous. "I can barely find the time to fill out the stupid annual appraisal form. The last thing I need is more paperwork!"

"I understand," Audrey responded gently. "Fortunately, I'm not talking about more paperwork. I'm talking about 2+2."

"What's 2+2?" Pauline's interest was suddenly piqued.

"Do you have your appointment calendar handy?" Audrey asked.

"Yes. But what century do you think this is? I don't carry a calendar. I carry a personal digital assistant. That way, I get to recharge one more gadget every night."

Audrey laughed. "What's on your schedule a week from next Tuesday?"

"Nothing that can't be changed."

"Great! I'm conducting a seminar on 2+2 at the civic center. I think you should be there. It could save you some major headaches."

Pauline took a deep breath. "I'll be there," she said.

KEY TAKEAWAYS

- Performance appraisal ratings cannot be relied upon as vehicles for effective feedback.

- Annual or even quarterly appraisals do not provide adequate opportunities for timely feedback.

- Employee perspective is key to improving personal and organizational performance—ask employees for their ideas as part of the feedback process.

FOUR

Celebrate Success and Encourage Improvement

Almost two weeks to the day since her disastrous performance appraisal of Percy, Pauline attended Audrey's seminar called "Formula 2+2: The Simple Solution for Successful Coaching." She took a seat as close to the podium as she could—she wanted to take in every word. She also hoped that by being near the front she'd be able to connect with Audrey during breaks.

She was interested to learn during the speaker's introduction that Audrey had just been promoted to professor of human resource management at a local university and served as a regular consultant and trainer for a number of Fortune 500 companies.

Audrey didn't immediately launch into a discussion of 2+2. Instead, she began with a discussion of how human behavior could best be influenced: "You have to get the brain's attention, provide feedback on what is being done well and what could be done better, and provide encouragement for the process of continuous improvement."

Attention, feedback, and encouragement are the pillars of successful coaching.

She makes it seem so simple, Pauline thought. *But like so many things that are simple and at the same time profound, it's one thing to describe that "simple" process and quite something else to make it happen.*

Audrey mentioned several traps of management practice that defy brain research. "So much of what we do is based on threat, and yet the brain doesn't function well under threat. So much of our feedback is delivered in the form of criticism, and yet the brain responds much more predictably to encouragement. And finally, so much of what we do is expedient, violating trust—when trust is the basis for the rapid positive shaping of behavior."

> Success is something to talk about— often!

Pauline raised her hand to make a comment. "You're right," she agreed. "I've found that most people are afraid of feedback. They say they want to hear how they are doing, but they are not open to frank discussions of their shortcomings. This is one of the factors that make performance appraisal discussions with my staff so painful. It is the one time of year when I can really give them some solid suggestions on how they can improve, but they are usually not too receptive to my observations."

"I used to experience the same frustration," Audrey replied. "I would use the performance appraisal as my time to correct a person's behavior, but my staff seemed to be tuning me out.

"I discovered that correcting behavior was only half of the manager's job. It was equally important that I recognized and reinforced what was going right.

"This is the discipline of 2+2. It forces us to take a balanced look at how our people are doing, placing equal emphasis on what they are doing well and what they might need to improve. For many managers, this is really quite revolutionary!

"In fact, there is a paradox here: my people needed more feedback on how they were doing, but they also needed more room to make mistakes.

"You see, behavioral change is most successful when feedback is offered and received in a positive environment where the trial-and-error approach is encouraged. We need to celebrate risk taking *and the mistakes* that often result.

> We need to celebrate risk taking *and the mistakes* that often result.

"It's a process. Feedback doesn't instantly enable a person to modify behavior or perfect a new skill. We have to give people the freedom to try and fail, then try again and succeed, if we hope to achieve the desired performance.

"For instance, it's almost impossible to learn to ride a bicycle without falling. Scraped elbows and knees are a necessary part of the learning process. Parents and friends help the process along by providing encouragement. Trial, error, and the resulting feedback lead to a very steep but positive learning curve.

"Learning to ride a bicycle simply by studying a manual—even a very good manual that describes the trial-and-error process—is basically impossible. The same is true in the classroom, in the workplace, on the battlefield, or on the playing field. Feedback and encouragement are the prime motivators of success. Without adequate feedback—fueled with encouragement for trial and error—we will not be able to fully develop the professional capacity of our teams.

"In fact, as managers, we need to take responsibility for celebrating our people's successes as seriously as we take responsibility for correcting their shortcomings."

As several members of the audience nodded in thoughtful agreement, Audrey continued, "To successfully carry out these dual responsibilities, managers need to put into practice the secret of *balance!* This is the pivotal secret of the 2+2 feedback system. When we come back from our break, I'll discuss this most crucial secret in more detail."

KEY TAKEAWAYS

- The brain reacts most positively to encouragement.
- Allow room for mistakes; encourage trial-and-error learning.
- Feedback is a natural and necessary part of learning.
- Feedback is as much about celebrating successes as it is about correcting problems!

FIVE

The Magic of Balance

After a short break, Pauline was just returning to her seat when Audrey began the second session.

"Practicing the art of *balance* is essential to effective feedback," Audrey suggested. "Let me state again that managers must take as much responsibility for reinforcing and celebrating good behavior as they take for correcting or improving problems in the workplace.

"We gain credibility by highlighting what is going well, as opposed to the common practice of simply dwelling on the failures of our people. If we simply note the areas in need of improvement, we lose credibility and we will be labeled as a negative person or complainer. By recognizing a person's strengths as well as areas in which improvement could be made, we reinforce the good work that is being done and in so doing make sure that the employee knows we have observed and appreciated his or her successes."

Audrey continued, "It has always been amazing to me to see how few managers truly understand the importance of balance. Most managers spend their time looking for what people are doing wrong and then jumping on them. While they think they are doing their best to promote good performance, this is clearly not the case. Ironically, research clearly shows that one of the best ways to stop behavior is to ignore it."

Audrey paused for emphasis, then stated somewhat dramatically, "Managers who focus on the mistakes their people make without recognizing their successes are unknowingly doing their best to stop their people from repeating what they do well!

"Performance is likely to improve the most when suggestions for improvement are balanced with compliments. While the precise number of two compliments and two suggestions is not the issue, balance is essential. The 2+2 framework provides the needed balance, initially as a supplement to more formal evaluation and perhaps later as an alternative to it.

Focusing on mistakes without recognizing excellence discourages repeated successes.

"As a result, managers, associates, and direct reports at all levels can be encouraged to participate in an informal practice of complimenting and suggesting. All levels of associates can be encouraged to be on the lookout for 'critical incidents' that are worth noting, either as effective behavior to be reinforced or less effective behavior for which alternatives or improvements can be suggested. Through the use of the 2+2 format, people at all levels can be encouraged to give feedback to their senior, junior, and peer colleagues. And to complete the circle, they should be alert for incidents of self-evaluation as well. With balance, they will be sure to reinforce and compliment the things that are going right as well as to identify areas where improvement is important."

Audrey paused for a moment, and raised hands were again visible around the room. She called on a man wearing jeans and a T-shirt sitting near Pauline who said, "I like the idea of 2+2, but I think that using compliments as a way of getting into a discussion of problems might be unethical. I don't like the idea of hidden agendas. Anyway, employees will know that the compliments are simply a prelude to that discussion."

Audrey had a ready answer from this. "It is important to understand that 2+2 compliments are not simply vehicles to get to the suggestions for improvement. Compliments and suggestions are equally important and will not be effective unless they are *both* offered with full sincerity. There are no hidden agendas. The 2+2 feedback system has two equally strong objectives: first, recognize successes so they can be reinforced and repeated, and second, encourage improvement in areas that are most in need of change."

> Compliments should not be used simply as a prelude to suggestions for improvement.

The man nodded and said, "That makes sense. I always like to be totally open and honest with my employees. Deception has no place in the workplace."

Audrey agreed, "Absolutely correct! The success of 2+2 depends very much on the trusting relationship between a manager and his or her team."

She then called on a woman who said, "This all seems kind of obvious. I'm in HR, and I've been doing something pretty much like this for years, even though I don't call it '2+2.'"

"Well," Audrey responded, "human resource consultants in general are often criticized for advocating the obvious. Some people even say that managing people is just common sense. Unfortunately, as I visit with managers and their people, I find that common sense is just not that widely practiced in the real world. The 2+2 system provides a framework to ensure that commonsense techniques are implemented."

The woman nodded in agreement and took her seat as Audrey continued. "In our society, more often the norm is to say nothing when things are going well and to call attention only to the problems or difficulties. The cultural roots that condition us to this practice run very deep. In fact, managers who give frequent compliments are sometimes thought to be 'sticky sweet' or even insincere. With 2+2, everyone expects and receives a balance of compliments and suggestions on a regular basis. A culture of helpful feedback is developed where complimenting and encouraging each other is the norm and the sting is removed from suggestions that are offered in a spirit of helpfulness.

"Formula 2+2 is the best way I know to achieve spirited performance from every member of your team!"

These ideas sound great, Pauline thought. But as she reflected on her disastrous run-in with Percy, it was not clear at all how these lofty principles had anything to do with day-to-day management problems and the disaster she was facing because of Percy's departure.

+ + +

As soon as the morning session ended, Audrey stepped down from the stage and immediately approached Pauline.

"Do you have plans for lunch?"

"No. In fact, if you hadn't asked me, I was going to ask you," Pauline admitted.

A few minutes later, as they sipped on their lemonades and waited to place their lunch orders, Audrey listened to Pauline vividly recount the details of Percy's overreaction to his performance appraisal.

"I'm not surprised by his reaction at all," Audrey told Pauline.

"You're kidding!" Pauline was somewhat irritated by Audrey's response. Obviously, Audrey had really climbed into her ivory tower along with all the other university types who had lots of theories but didn't have to manage a sales staff.

Then, much to Pauline's surprise, Audrey added, "It certainly is frustrating when our people cannot read our minds."

Pauline was dumbfounded. "What do you mean cannot read our minds? Far from asking them to read my mind, I have spelled out very clearly what each of my salespeople is expected to accomplish during the year. I use their annual performance appraisal and goal-setting sessions to do this. They sign off on their goals and understand very clearly what is expected of them. On top of that, when problems get to a certain level of severity, I meet with them and clearly outline my concerns in a kind and straightforward manner."

"How often do you praise them for doing a good job? And why don't you approach them immediately when you see a problem?" asked Audrey.

Pauline thought for a minute. "I'm not really sure, but I probably thank my staff quite frequently. Certainly they know what their goals are and, as long as they are on track, they know I appreciate what they are doing. I'm really not a complainer. I resort to giving negative feedback only when I feel it's absolutely necessary. After all, I don't want to look like I'm constantly griping or being too picky."

"Although it may be unintentional, it sounds as though you are asking your people to be mind readers. All employees need regular feedback to help maintain their morale and keep them focused on the required tasks. As I mentioned earlier, I've found that people are happiest when their bosses effectively recognize what they are doing well and not just point out what they need to improve."

Pauline wondered what she could do to give her people the support and feedback required to lessen their need for mind-reading skills. After all, she had to admit that "psychic" was not part of her staff's job description.

"Our session this afternoon will give more insights into how the 2+2 coaching and feedback system works," Audrey continued. "It has revolutionized every company that has tried it. It is as easy and as hard as 2+2."

"As easy and as hard?" Pauline wondered aloud.

Audrey explained: "The 2+2 system is both simple and powerful. It provides a framework and philosophy for managing informal or formal feedback to people. With 2+2, some managers have even done away with their traditional performance appraisal system altogether."

"How is that possible?" asked Pauline. "Isn't the formal performance appraisal a necessary evil required of all managers?"

"If that's your view of your current performance appraisal system, I'm even more confident you will find 2+2 an effective and attractive vehicle for giving your people the feedback they need."

"Tell me more," said Pauline.

"Many managers believe that the key to effective leadership is simply to get out and visit with their people. Some people call this 'face-to-face management' or 'management by wandering around.' As critical as personal contact is, it's still not enough.

"What may be missing in 'management by wandering around' is effective feedback. We need to ensure that we regularly build systematic and timely feedback into that personal contact with our people. The more effective managers intuitively integrate feedback discussions in their routine interactions with people. Sad to say, most managers are not so adept."

KEY TAKEAWAYS

- Reinforce people's strengths as well as suggest opportunities for improvement.

- Provide intrinsic reward through recognition.

- Increase the likelihood of a positive response to suggestions for improvement.

- Do not use compliments simply as a prelude to suggestions.

- Enhance credibility and trust by sharing balanced feedback with your people.

SIX

The Importance of Timeliness

"How many times," Audrey continued, "have you heard a manager say in frustration, 'I don't know what happened! Last year, I sat down with one of my staff. We agreed upon some reasonable goals. She looked me in the eye and promised to accomplish them. We even shook hands! Now, it's performance appraisal time and she hasn't accomplished her goals. I'm going to have to give her a bad performance appraisal.'"

Pauline smiled knowingly. "Sounds familiar," she said.

"Where was the midcourse correction?" Audrey asked. "Remember the lesson of *Luna 1*? Scientists took their best aim and shot a rocket at the moon. At some point along the way, the rocket drifted off course. The scientists probably slapped their knees and said, 'Darn it, missed the moon!' And that was that.

"Yet very soon after that first attempt, scientists developed the capability to provide timely feedback in the form of midcourse corrections to rockets they fired at the moon and elsewhere. This made hitting the moon relatively simple and much more certain."

Pauline nodded. "It's hard to believe that it was only ten years after *Luna 1* that *Apollo 11* landed people on the moon and brought them safely home."

"Yes, it is," responded Audrey. "But what's amazing is that managers who rely on infrequent performance appraisals as their primary source of feedback are basically still doing the same thing as those early rocket scientists. They use a goal-setting discussion to aim people, they launch them with a handshake, and then stand back to see what happens. By the time the performance appraisal comes around, these people have veered off course and the manager says, 'Darn it! Missed again!'"

"So people need midcourse corrections, too." Pauline said.

"That's it exactly!" said Audrey. "Somewhere between the casual thank-you and the annual performance appraisal lies the manager's need to let people know what they are doing well and what they must improve.

> Formula 2+2: somewhere between the casual thank-you and the annual appraisal.

"Powerful feedback has a short shelf life. Research shows very clearly that our biggest opportunity to reinforce or change behavior is very close to the time the behavior occurs. When someone gets too far off course, it becomes much more difficult to bring them back on target. That's why the next secret of 2+2 is *timeliness*."

"It seems so obvious when you put it that way," Pauline said. "Providing people with timely feedback helps them improve and at the same time keeps them on course!"

"And consider this," Audrey continued. "Quick feedback also facilitates a steeper learning curve for people. Imagine how long it would take for people to learn to ride a bicycle if they had to wait for their next annual performance appraisal to find out how they had done on their last try? People learn to ride bicycles quickly because they get immediate—and often painful—feedback on each attempt to ride. This allows them to conduct many experiments in a short time. Managers who rely on annual or even quarterly performance appraisals as a primary feedback mechanism are not conveying a sense of urgency for improvement to their people. By the time the feedback is delivered, many issues will have been long forgotten and the opportunity for improvement lost forever."

"I think I'm beginning to understand what you meant by mind reading," Pauline observed. "I've been waiting until matters got really bad before talking with my staff. I thought I was giving them room for improvement, but I was actually giving them rope with which to hang themselves."

"You're not alone. Many well-intentioned managers—hoping to give their people space—shy away from giving adequate feedback on a regular basis. As a result, people may actually stop doing what they do well and may continue to do some of the things they are doing poorly. The longer the lag between the action and the feedback, the less effective the feedback will be.

> The longer the delay, the less effective the feedback.

"Of course, at some point, even a well-intentioned manager finally gets fed up and explodes. More commonly—and even worse—he or she may let the frustration build until the annual performance review. No wonder most people and their managers don't look forward to performance appraisals!"

"The truth is, I've decided that the only thing worse than going to the dentist is conducting a performance appraisal," said Pauline.

"Not a bad analogy. Why is it you don't like going to the dentist?" Audrey asked rhetorically. "For most people, it is because they are embarrassed that they haven't done their daily brushing and flossing and they are worried that their teeth have decayed. A patient who brushes and flosses in a timely fashion has much less to fear."

"I am faithful in my brushing and flossing," Pauline offered. "I just don't like someone in a mask probing around in my mouth with sharp objects."

Audrey laughed. "Regular feedback won't solve all the problems, but when supervisors don't keep up with their managerial 'brushing and flossing,' they develop major problems over time. That, of course, leads to lots of proverbial sharp objects."

"Please!" Pauline said, feigning pain. "I don't even want to talk about it!"

"It's at about that point that many managers fall into the SEWER trap," Audrey continued.

"The sewer trap?"

"It's an acronym. It means 'Silent Except When EnRaged.'"

"I can see how managers fall into that trap. I've done it myself," Pauline responded. "How do I avoid it?"

"Don't wait too long to give your people feedback. Some managers are too lazy to give feedback. For many, it's simply their default style and perhaps a reflection of the bad example set by their own supervisors. Others actually think this is good management, and some simply feel uncomfortable saying 'thank you' to someone for a routine good job. It is probably safe to say that whenever performance appraisals result in shock or surprise, the manager has not provided his or her people with adequate feedback along the way."

> Whenever performance appraisals result in surprise, the manager has failed.

"You know," Pauline admitted, "I probably don't spend as much time as I should talking with my staff and finding opportunities to compliment ordinary good performance. But it is so hard to plan in advance. How do you structure the time into the day to schedule meetings with all of your people?"

"I have found," Audrey responded, "that not providing good feedback is what actually *costs* me a lot of time. As an example, a few years ago—before I began using 2+2—I was sure that one of my new salespeople, Simon, was losing customers because he didn't call them frequently enough. I hoped he might improve, so I decided to wait until the next performance appraisal to tell him about my concerns. Unfortunately, by then seventeen of our long-term customers had moved much of their business to other suppliers."

"Whew! That must have had a disastrous impact on your business."

"Yes, it did," Audrey replied. "But I got involved at that point and worked with Simon and the rest of my team to recover as many of those customers as possible. We earned most of them back, but I spent a lot of time undoing the damage. I know that if I had acted sooner, I could have avoided the whole mess. In fact, a twenty-minute conversation is probably all it would have taken. As it turned out, Simon went on to become a great team member, but initially he needed quite a bit of guidance since he was relatively new to sales."

"Your story reminds me of some of the times that I probably should have stepped in earlier than I did," Pauline said. "Reminds me of a saying I heard years ago that goes something like this: 'It costs one dollar to prevent a problem, ten dollars to fix a problem, and one hundred dollars to repair the damage if the problem is left untended.'"

"That's the truth," Audrey said, "That's why *timeliness* is so important. It makes it easier to help people stay on course!

"Timeliness can be achieved either formally through scheduled meetings or spontaneously whenever the need arises. Most managers use a combination of both. In either case, be sure to choose a time and place that will be comfortable for the employee to receive the feedback you have to offer. This will make it more likely that your compliments and suggestions will be well received.

"Thanks to regular feedback, your people will always know where they stand."

"So exactly how does 2+2 work?" Pauline asked eagerly. "Our afternoon session will answer your question," Audrey assured her.

KEY TAKEAWAYS

- Feedback must be given regularly.

- The closer feedback can be given to the time the behavior occurs, the better.

- Time conversations to maximize receptivity to compliments as well as suggestions.

- Share feedback in an appropriate setting.

- Timely feedback avoids surprises during formal performance appraisal discussions.

- Avoid the SEWER trap!

SEVEN

The Spirit of 2+2

The seminar reconvened at precisely 1:30 p.m. Pauline was seated in her chair near the front, pad and pen ready to record every nugget of wisdom Audrey was about to throw her way.

"Formula 2+2 is a very effective and powerful way to offer feedback to people," Audrey began. "It can be used anytime you want to have a formal and systematic discussion of goals, performance, or other issues. But the real benefit is that it can be used to provide informal feedback anytime, at the request of either one of your people or yourself. Very simply, 2+2 involves five basic secrets: balance, timeliness, focus, specificity, and follow-up, all presented in the context of a low-risk and supportive environment. We'll be talking about how each of these secrets can transform the way you give feedback to your people.

THE FIVE SECRETS OF 2+2
1 Balance
2 Timeliness
3 Focus
4 Specificity
5 Follow-up

"In many businesses, the typical performance appraisal has become much more complicated than it needs to be. It's so overlaid with forms and procedures that many managers detest going through the process. In fact, at lunch today, a friend of mine described the performance appraisal as the rough equivalent of a trip to the dentist."

Chuckles rippled through the room as Audrey continued.

"The essential purpose of the performance appraisal, or PA as I sometimes call it, has been lost in the midst of bureaucratic forms and annual meetings that often result in hurt feelings and tears. Its original purpose of providing meaningful feedback to employees has largely been lost.

"This is exactly where 2+2 can help: 2+2 encourages managers to embrace giving and receiving feedback as a potentially joyous and regular part of their job."

Joyous? Pauline's naturally skeptical mind had some trouble connecting with that statement. She had heard performance appraisals and feedback discussions referred to in many different ways, none of which had ever incorporated the word "joyous."

As if anticipating the audience's skepticism, Audrey continued, "While it may seem hard to imagine, feedback to your people can be very positive and well received. In fact, feedback should be as much a celebration of successes as it is a correction of problems.

> Feedback should be as much a celebration of successes as it is a correction of problems.

"But for this to happen, we need to adopt a new spirit of helpfulness and a vision that feedback is not just a process of correcting and criticizing poor behavior, but is instead a process of encouragement. As you come to understand the spirit of 2+2, you will find that it involves a true spirit of encouragement, where recognition of a job well done is as much a part of the feedback process as are helpful suggestions for improvement.

"In too many organizations, the culture of feedback is very negative. Employees often feel as if they have to surrender their dignity at the door because they work for a boss who has trouble communicating how they are performing.

"Compliments are few and far between and employees report feeling 'demolished' rather than encouraged by the criticism they receive from their managers. The spirit of 2+2 promotes a positive and helpful culture of feedback that allows employees to retain their pride and dignity even as they receive regular feedback on their performance.

"Based upon my past experience, I am sure that some of you already have this spirit—even if you don't yet know it. Many others here will be able to catch the spirit and allow it to transform their vision of what a manager is and how managers and their staff can work together to achieve high performance!"

Audrey continued. "Armed with this joyous spirit, the 2+2 approach to feedback is very straightforward. It involves offering two compliments on effective performance in tandem with two suggestions for improvement. The 2+2 format disciplines a manager to provide balanced feedback that is focused and helpful.

"If you try the simple 2+2 formula, I guarantee that you will be amazed at how well your feedback is received. At first, some of the joy I referred to may simply be the pleasant surprise expressed by people who are not used to receiving sincere compliments from a supervisor. As you continue to practice 2+2, the joy will come from the meaningful and comfortable exchange of perspectives between you and your staff on an ongoing basis.

When you use 2+2 systematically, the annual performance appraisal form will become an occasional summary of the regular feedback you have given to your people. The result is that your employees won't be shocked by any unanticipated feedback in the annual performance appraisal because you have provided helpful midcourse guidance to them on a continuing basis."

Audrey paused briefly as she scanned the audience. "I can see puzzled looks on some of your faces, so why don't we take a few minutes for questions?"

A number of hands shot into the air.

A young man sitting in the middle of the room stood up and asked a bit nervously, "Does the spirit of 2+2 mean that we have to be charismatic to give great feedback? I'm not a particularly dynamic manager, and I definitely don't think of myself as charismatic."

"Not at all," responded Audrey. "You raise an excellent point. The spirit of 2+2 is about honesty and being genuine more than it is about charisma. The success of our feedback is determined much more by a sincere desire to help our people than it is determined by our dynamism."

Looking relieved, the man thanked Audrey and sat down.

Audrey directed her attention to a well-dressed man sitting off to one side.

"My days are already very full," the man said. "I really don't have time for more programs, systems, or procedures. Why would I want to get involved in this complicated 2+2 system?"

"Good question," Audrey acknowledged. "And the answer is, 2+2 isn't all that complicated or time intensive. A key feature of effective 2+2 is the informality of a feedback session. It can just 'happen' as part of your daily routine. A 'session' may involve nothing more than a passing conversation as a manager interacts with a direct report. Of course, a feedback session may also be much more structured. Therefore, it is important that everyone understand the secrets of 2+2.

"Formula 2+2 is not so much a new project as it is a new way of communicating during the time you already spend with your people. It is an investment of a manager's time that can actually save a lot of time in the long run. It gives managers a natural way to celebrate successes and address problems in 'real time.' Because it is so simple, it's easy to hold a 2+2 conversation anytime one of your people does something noteworthy."

> Formula 2+2 is not a new project but rather a new way of communicating.

The man nodded and sat down, and raised hands again filled the air. Audrey called on a woman near the center aisle.

"How do we keep the discussion from getting nasty and the people from getting defensive? This always seems to happen with many of my staff when I conduct their annual performance reviews. They think it's one-sided—that I'm just coming down on them."

Audrey thought for a moment. "Remember the spirit of 2+2, which emphasizes helpfulness and encouragement. If you approach feedback with this spirit, your people are much more likely to respond in a positive manner, with less defensiveness and more openness.

"Balance is also helpful in this regard. If you can focus on areas of success as well as opportunities for improvement, your people will be less likely to feel attacked and more likely to trust the quality of your feedback.

"Let's take a short break and when we come back, I'll share the next 2+2 secret with you."

KEY TAKEAWAYS

The Spirit of 2+2 includes

- Joy.
- Helpfulness.
- Encouragement.
- Sincere concern for people.
- Celebration of success!

**A SPECIAL MESSAGE FROM
BUZZ ALDRIN, ASTRONAUT,
APOLLO 11—THE MAN
WHO SAID "MAGNIFICENT
DESOLATION" AS HE TOOK
HIS FIRST STEPS ON THE
MOON JULY 20, 1969.**

CONGRATULATIONS on passing the midpoint on your journey to learn how to give great 2+2 feedback. Well done—even though you still have a ways to go.

On our way to the moon we received constant feedback from Mission Control on all aspects of our mission. It gave us the means and the confidence to succeed. By the way, from time to time we could have used even more information about what was going on— we certainly had our nervous moments.

Everyone needs regular updates on how they are doing—2+2 is an effective way to give your people the encouragement and confidence they need for success.

Good luck as you continue your journey!

EIGHT

The Power of Focus

When people were once again seated, Audrey continued her presentation: "Before we go any further," she said, "I want to emphasize the secret of focus.

"It is well known that behavior is more likely to be influenced if feedback addresses no more than one or two elements at any given time. In light of this, it makes no sense to overwhelm a person with a huge laundry list of successes and failures—most of which would likely be forgotten. However, this is exactly what happens in many performance appraisal meetings. People often feel like they are facing a fire hose as their manager quickly and superficially runs through a large list of performance criteria.

"Instead, 2+2 focuses the feedback in such a way that only two of the most important compliments and suggestions are covered. Other issues— positive or negative—even if important, can wait until another time. With 2+2, time and attention are reserved for the most important issues only."

"Fire-hose" feedback is rarely effective.

Audrey moved over to a large screen upon which a bell-shaped curve was being projected. "Focus directs our attention to the 'tails' of our people's performance. The typical person engages in a wide variety of behaviors on a daily basis and performs most of these with competence. Conceptually, we can illustrate people's behavior as falling on a basic bell-shaped curve."

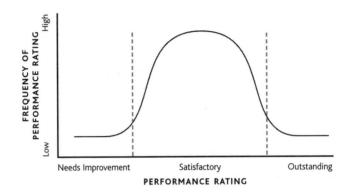

Pointing to the diagram on the screen, Audrey continued, "As you can see, the behavior on the left side of the curve is the lowest-rated behavior. This is where potential problems may lie. Note that for the typical person, there are relatively few instances of poorly rated behavior. The curve shows that most of a person's behavior is rated as acceptable but not outstanding. While we might like to see some of that behavior improve also, improvement in these areas is a lower priority than is the behavior indicated by the left tail."

Audrey then moved to the other side of the screen and pointed to the right tail of the curve. "Here at the other end of the curve are a few behaviors that are outstanding. These are the priority areas to recognize, reward, and reinforce as being highly valued. Other areas further back on the curve may be worthy of recognition as well, but in order to really focus the person's attention on the most important areas of success, we will wait until a later time to discuss those."

A man near the back of the room raised his hand with a question: "What do I do if 2+2 is not enough? What if one employee has so many important issues that I start falling behind in my feedback?"

"In that case, I recommend that you consider increasing the frequency of your 2+2 conversations with that employee," Audrey replied. "*Saving up* feedback is not the concept of 2+2. If you find that important issues are not being addressed in a timely fashion, you may want to set up a weekly or even more frequent 2+2 schedule. Take care, however, because at some point, too many 2+2 conversations will begin to feel like the fire hose or laundry list that 2+2 is trying to avoid and could become counterproductive. This is where your judgment as a manager becomes critical."

The man smiled his thanks as a young woman sitting next to Pauline raised her hand. "I'd be worried that I'm not giving a comprehensive assessment if I ignore that large middle area."

Audrey acknowledged that this was an important point. "Of course, we don't want to perpetually ignore the many good but less outstanding aspects of our people's performance—performance that falls somewhere in the mushy middle of the performance curve. Our daily interactions with people are a perfect time to find informal opportunities to comment on those behaviors as well. Keep in mind that it is not the purpose of 2+2 to provide people with a comprehensive assessment of their performance. It is intentionally designed to force you to focus on the most important performance areas.

> Formula 2+2 is not intended to be comprehensive in any one session.

"But you raise an important issue relevant to the theory of 2+2. Multiple 2+2 conversations allow ample opportunity for rating individual behaviors. If a performance characteristic is not covered after there have been many opportunities to do so, it is safe for a person to assume that it lies somewhere in the middle of the curve.

"Remember that 2+2 is a metaphor for *balance* and *focus*. Compliments and suggestions for improvements are balanced with approximately equal emphasis. While the number *two* is in no way required, the principle of focusing your feedback on the one or two most important successes you want to reinforce as well as the one or two most important opportunities for improvement will be critical to your success."

When the seminar concluded, Pauline again approached Audrey.

"I liked what you had to say. I can see how 2+2 could become my best tool to coach and encourage my people, as well as to fix what is 'broken.' I think I'll have to start slow, though."

"That's the best approach," Audrey agreed. "Sudden, unexpected change is not always welcome."

"I have one request, though," Pauline asked without hesitation. "Would you be willing to mentor me as I try it out?"

"Feel free to call me anytime," Audrey offered as they made their way toward the exit.

KEY TAKEAWAYS

- Highlight and encourage your employees' most outstanding behavior.

- Identify and discuss priority areas for change and improvement.

- Avoid intimidating and easily forgotten laundry lists of behavior.

NINE

Getting 2+2 Up and Running

When Pauline returned to work the next day—fresh out of Audrey's seminar—she was more than a little excited. The 2+2 program was something she wanted to try right away.

As was her practice, she arrived at the office at 6:30 a.m., a good half hour before any of the others usually came in. As she settled in for some early morning work at her desk, she determined that she would first try out 2+2 on Chad, a relatively recent hire who had already demonstrated substantial strengths.

When Chad arrived in his office, Pauline immediately approached him. "Mind if I sit down for a few minutes?" she asked. "I'd like to talk with you about a couple of things."

Chad was a bit wary. He had heard all about the performance appraisal Pauline had given Percy, and he was in no mood for any kind of run-in. "I have a client report that you wanted me to finish today," he began, "so unless it's really urgent, could it possibly wait until tomorrow?"

Pauline shrugged and replied, "No problem." But on her way out of his office, she was feeling disappointed that she hadn't gotten to test her knowledge of 2+2.

Since she was already out and about, she decided to drop in on Sydnay, thinking that perhaps she could use 2+2 on her.

She popped her head in Sydnay's office and asked if she could visit for a few minutes. Although Sydnay was on the phone with a customer, she waved Pauline in to take a seat.

When the phone call ended, Pauline immediately launched into two compliments: "I just wanted to compliment you on the good work you have been doing over the past several months. Secondly, I've heard you've been much more productive. What an improvement! Meanwhile, I'd also like to raise a couple of issues that have been on my mind for some time. I really think you need to spend more time with customers. Also, I'd like to see you invest more time with your staff."

Pauline was pleased that she had offered two compliments and two suggestions so easily. This 2+2 was a snap! It had allowed her to have a meaningful discussion with Sydnay and get some issues out on the table that had been bothering her for some time. To Pauline's surprise, Sydnay was obviously agitated and came off as a bit angry. Pauline tried to engage in a bit of small talk with her, but the conversation seemed strained. After two or three minutes, Sydnay got up and said that she was sorry to have to end the encounter, but she was in serious danger of missing a tight client deadline. "Perhaps we can talk more later."

Pauline was disappointed in the meeting. It was clear that 2+2 had not worked the way she had anticipated. She had expected that the 2+2 session could lead to a longer, more detailed discussion. Instead, in her very first attempt, her direct report had essentially kicked her out of the office before any problem-solving discussions could take place. Pauline was beginning to realize that 2+2 was going to require some trial-and-error learning before she got it right.

> Formula 2+2 requires trial-and-error learning.

Upon returning to her office, Pauline called Audrey and described what had happened. Audrey listened carefully and then asked Pauline how she had prepared for the meeting.

"Prepared?" asked Pauline. "I thought 2+2 was supposed to be very informal."

"It is," said Audrey, "but it may be helpful to set the scene before starting to use 2+2. For many managers, 2+2 involves a significant change in the style of interaction they have with their people. Because of this, it is probably best to talk about 2+2 as a concept with your people first so they know what you are trying to do. Otherwise, such a major change in your behavior may be disconcerting.

> Don't keep it secret—be open about 2+2.

"Also, and equally importantly, you have to think ahead about what you are going to discuss. Remember the secret of focus. You want to prioritize your feedback so that you cover the strongest and weakest aspects of the person's behavior. In order to do this, you need to do your homework. Assess possible points you might raise and consider whether you have really focused on the two most important compliments and the two most powerful suggestions. This doesn't have to take long, but it can very well make the difference between success and failure in your feedback conversations.

"And after you identify the points you want to raise, I strongly recommend you build *specificity* into your comments. Specificity helps ensure that your employees understand your feedback and sets the scene for a meaningful discussion with them."

KEY TAKEAWAYS

- Effective feedback requires the building of a trusting relationship between manager and direct report.

- Effective feedback involves preparation.

- Levels of receptivity will, at first, vary among people.

- Explicit discussion of the 2+2 concept with people beforehand may make it easier to start up a 2+2 program.

The Need for Specificity

"Specificity?" Pauline frowned. "I gave Sydnay two specific compliments and two specific suggestions for improvement. I'm not sure what more I could have done."

"Are you sure she really understood what you were complimenting and what you were suggesting should be improved?" Audrey asked. "Did you provide some specific examples she could relate to?"

"Not really, but that's partly because she was so quick to cut the meeting short."

"For 2+2 feedback to be effective, you need to be able to provide specific examples of the behavior you are describing. In addition, you should be very specific about the reasons your suggestion or compliment is important. Without specific examples, the person may miss your point. Then he or she may become defensive or, in some cases, even hostile instead of acting on the feedback."

"I certainly sensed that," Pauline admitted. "Do you really think it's because I didn't communicate my concerns specifically enough?"

"That could have been part of your problem with your first try. Think back about what you said during your 2+2 conversation."

"Hmm, I see what you mean. I mentioned that Sydnay needed to spend more time with customers, but I didn't say why or give any examples of how less time spent with customers had created problems."

"I'd suggest that you try 2+2 again," said Audrey. "But this time do more homework before you have your meeting. Even if you have to bring some notes to the meeting, the importance of balance, focus, and specificity warrants the extra effort."

"I understand."

"When I prepare myself for a 2+2 conversation," Audrey continued, "there's another important thought that I try to keep in my mind."

"What's that?" Pauline asked.

"It's simply this: *even well-intentioned suggestions can be taken very negatively.* Research has clearly shown that compliments and reprimands are not received with equal attention. It often takes as many as four or more compliments to balance out one reprimand. People are likely to be offended or become defensive if your entire objective is to simply offer an equal number of compliments and reprimands."

"Then why not practice 4+1?" asked Pauline.

Audrey laughed. "The exact numbers aren't what's really important. The key is to tilt the conversation toward the positive. In most cases, the two-to-two ratio is completely effective. You simply need to think ahead about how you can keep the conversation positive. You might want to underline the positive compliments by repeating them or saying them in different ways. And then, if most of your suggestions can be made in the

> "Bad job" is not effective feedback—give specific examples!

> "Good job" is not effective feedback—give specific examples!

form of positive and helpful ideas instead of personal criticism, you should be able to maintain a balance within the 2+2 formula. Part of the philosophy of this system is that real-time feedback should take place as part of positive and encouraging interactions with people. A mistake most managers tend to make is to assume that a suggestion for change or improvement has to be delivered as criticism.

"If, in rare instances, criticism is unavoidable, be aware that much complimentary conversation may have to take place to offset the hurt feelings that criticism may cause. But remember, too, if compliments are not sincere, they are worse than none at all!"

Pauline nodded in agreement. "I know exactly what you're saying. It takes me a long time to get over the effects of negative comments from a manager or from a friend."

"It's that way with most people," Audrey said.

"Interesting," Pauline said. "I didn't realize that something that initially sounded so simple would require so much thought. I guess I'm going to have to spend more time planning before I use 2+2."

+ + +

That evening, Pauline spent an hour or more preparing to relaunch 2+2 in her organization. She decided that the first step would be to discuss 2+2 with her people at the next regularly scheduled staff meeting and speak frankly with them about what she was trying to accomplish. She also resolved that she would not enter into a 2+2 discussion with anyone unless she felt she was prepared for the conversation.

Pauline outlined several simple points she would follow before any 2+2 feedback session.

1. Always have at least one positive compliment and one suggestion for improvement to make during the meeting (balance).

2. Always have specific examples ready to back up each of the compliments and suggestions (specificity).

3. Evaluate the compliments and suggestions to be sure that the ones chosen are indeed the highest-priority issues to raise at that time (focus).

4. Explicitly schedule a regular 2+2 session with each employee so that he or she will not be caught by surprise.

5. Continually modify this checklist based on experience gained and new approaches learned.

Two days later, Pauline conducted the monthly staff meeting. Everything went fairly well for about the first half hour. Sales figures had improved a little—not to the extent that all of them had hoped for, but nonetheless close enough to the target that all were optimistic that they would be able to reach this year's objectives.

Pauline went out of her way to express appreciation for everyone's hard work, and she exhorted her team to focus on further improvement during the remaining months of the year. She offered several specific ideas she thought would be helpful as the staff prepared to enter what was historically the busiest time of year.

Toward the end of the meeting, Pauline announced her plan to begin using 2+2. She acknowledged that her feedback to them in the past had not been as effective as it should have been. She said that she now realized that reliance on the formal performance appraisal system was not sufficient. While it served as a formal way to document observed behavior, it did very little to offer them the recognition they deserved. And the current system didn't provide opportunities for immediate midcourse corrections when inevitable problems arose. She emphasized that 2+2 would provide a vehicle for conversations about how things were going. She talked about the philosophy of 2+2 and added that while she would start using 2+2 herself, she would eventually expect her staff to use it with one another as well.

Although Pauline tried to encourage discussion, her salespeople appeared anxious for the meeting to end. As they left the meeting, Chad turned to Sydnay and said, "Oh boy, what are we in for now?"

Sydnay said, "I think I have some idea. A couple of days ago, Pauline came in and launched into some general compliments that were simply an unusual prelude to her typical criticisms: I need to sell more and work harder. Chad, I've heard these before and I don't need to hear them again. If 2+2 is a code word for more unfounded criticism, I'm going to follow Percy out the door and start looking for a new job."

Chad agreed. "She stopped by my office a couple of days ago, too. I knew she was going to attack me for something, so I told her I was under deadline pressure."

"Well, that was probably the truth," Sydnay observed somberly. "When *aren't* we under deadline pressure?"

Chad was getting even more agitated. "Won't she ever learn? We know our jobs better than anyone, and complaining will not help us do better. And the last thing we need is to start getting on each other's case as well. Can you imagine my coming into your office to give you feedback on your job? Ridiculous! We need to spend more time working with customers, not harassing each other."

"I agree," Sydnay said. "I wish Percy were still around. He'd know how to handle this."

KEY TAKEAWAYS

Support feedback with specific examples of behavior that

- Highlight specific incidents.

- Represent the issue at hand.

- Are timed for maximum impact.

ELEVEN

2+2: Take Two

Three weeks later, an unexpected visitor poked his head in Pauline's door. It was Percy!

Pauline's jaw dropped. "What are you doing here? I thought you'd have relocated to New Orleans by now."

"Naw. I really like the jazz and the blues, but the food is way too spicy for me," he replied with a wink.

"It's so good to see you!" Pauline exclaimed as she threw all caution to the wind and gave him a big hug. "Come in. Sit down."

"Thanks. Listen, Pauline, there's something I have to tell you—"

"There's something I have to tell you first," Pauline interrupted. "I am really sorry about what happened between us. Worse than that, I confess, I'm ashamed. I never should have handled your performance appraisal the way I did. You were too valuable a team member for me to just let you walk."

Percy was visibly moved. "Thanks, Pauline. The truth is, I came here to ask you if there would still be a position here that I could fill. I realize this company is where I belong."

Without a moment's hesitation, Pauline called the HR department and set everything in motion. Percy would once again be a part of her team.

+ + +

The following week, it occurred to Pauline that in the midst of all the commotion of bringing Percy back on board, she had completely ignored the implementation of 2+2. In addition to spontaneous 2+2 conversations, she had wanted to establish a regular rotating schedule that would allow her to meet with each person at least once every month, but now she was already behind.

Pauline settled behind her desk and decided that her first encounter under her "new" approach to 2+2 should be with Percy. *After that disastrous annual performance review, he'll see 2+2 as a positive change,* she thought. She dialed his extension.

Unfortunately, Percy had already been briefed on the "2+2 thing" by Chad and Sydnay, and he was armed with excuses.

"I'm really busy, Pauline. I'm trying to get back in good stead with all of my customers, and I have to gather information on some of the recent product enhancements. And my office systems aren't up to speed, either."

Percy suggested that they put off the 2+2 meeting until the end of the quarter—about two months later.

Pauline responded that getting 2+2 up and running was a priority with her and that she really needed him to make time in the next two weeks. Percy agreed to meet with her in his office the following week.

At the agreed-upon time, Pauline appeared in the doorway of Percy's office and asked if she could come in. Percy cleared a stack of papers from a chair so she could sit down. Pauline began by asking how things were going. She wondered whether he had found the new sales brochure effective. Percy said he liked the new brochure and indicated that customers were responding very favorably to the attractive presentation of the company's products. After a few minutes of fairly comfortable small talk, Pauline steered the conversation toward 2+2.

She thanked Percy for making the time to meet with her and assured him that the meeting would not take more than a few minutes. She also confided in Percy that she was a little nervous because this was the first 2+2 conversation she had conducted since the staff meeting in which she had announced the program. Since he had not been at that meeting, she asked him if he knew anything about 2+2. He assured her that he did.

Then Pauline told Percy that she had high hopes that the 2+2 concept could really help improve the quality of feedback taking place in the company.

As she launched into the 2+2 feedback conversation, she began by telling Percy how impressed she was with his successes since he had returned to the company. "You're already doing 14 percent better than you were when you left us. You really seem to have turned the corner in your district. I know that our competitors have been saturating the area with local advertising, and your sales figures are a testimony to your effectiveness in the field. You not only came back to the company, you staged a great comeback!"

> Don't do all the talking— listen to your people, too!

She then gave Percy a chance to talk about his accomplishments by asking how he had pulled it off. Percy's face immediately lit up as he described how he had initiated a combination telephone and site visit campaign to be sure that each of his customers had renewed personal contact from him. Pauline took some notes on a variety of ideas and told Percy that she was going to share his ideas with other members of the sales team.

Then Pauline mentioned how happy she was with the way Percy had introduced the new R-5 product into his area. In a very short time, Percy had sold more units than had any other salesperson in the company. Percy was visibly pleased that she had recognized this accomplishment. He had, after all, worked extremely hard to raise customer awareness of the new features offered on the R-5.

Pauline then said that she had a couple of suggestions to offer to Percy. While his overall sales were impressive, a couple of sectors in his district still seemed to be lagging. She pointed out that the numbers for his heavy industrial customers had steadily declined both before his departure and since his return—that, after several years of growth. She asked if he had any idea why this was happening. Percy responded that the heavy industrial customers were becoming more selective about their suppliers and he had found that his intensive efforts to court their business resulted in fewer sales than equal efforts in the light industrial and consumer markets. During recent months—and especially since his return—the attitude of the heavy industrial customers was such that he had pretty much written them off in favor of efforts to build other market niches. He would certainly accept their orders, but he wasn't going to go out of his way to sell to them.

Pauline said that she had heard similar stories from some of the other managers at the annual meeting. However, many of the salespeople were finding that the real problem was that the discounting structure in their industry had become increasingly cutthroat. These salespeople had negotiated with their managers to match the competitors' discounts in return for a longer-term contract. Sales were actually up in the heavy industrial market in some areas of the country.

Percy was intrigued by this news. He had assumed that such an aggressive pricing policy was not acceptable to the company and had not even bothered to ask. He told Pauline that if she would give him the authority to match competitors' discounts—with the provision that customers agree to a longer-term contract—he would be happy to give them another try. Pauline was pleased with this response and told him to go for it.

"There's one other issue I want to touch on briefly," Pauline added. "Last week, I sent you an e-mail and asked you to include Ginny on an R-5 sales call. To my knowledge, you still haven't done this. She isn't up to speed with the new technology yet and could really benefit from your quick grasp of this product's features and benefits. Could you let her know when you go on an R-5 call in the next few days? This would really help her."

Percy responded, "No problem. I had meant to invite her but have just been too busy. I'll make sure I give her a call today."

"Thanks," said Pauline. "I'm sure there will be a time soon when Ginny will be able to help you out in some way."

After a few minutes of small talk, Pauline asked Percy if there was anything she could do to help him do his job better or make his life at work easier. Percy replied that nothing came to mind. With that, Pauline was on her way out his door.

As she headed back to her office, she glanced at her watch and was amazed that so much had been accomplished in a twenty-five-minute meeting. She had actually enjoyed meeting with Percy, and even her suggestions had gone over well. She could hardly wait to meet Sydnay the next day!

At the same time, Percy was sitting at his desk reflecting on what had just happened. Pauline had not criticized him at all. Rather, she had been downright complimentary much of the time. And when she had offered her so-called suggestions, they had been in the spirit of helpfulness and problem solving, not anger or frustration.

Maybe this 2+2 stuff isn't so bad after all, he thought. *Sure beats that annual performance review.*

Percy used the last half hour of the workday to set up a series of appointments with his old heavy industrial customers, many of whom he hadn't seen for some time.

+ + +

Three days later, Pauline was in her office reflecting on her successful relaunch of 2+2. Her meeting with Percy had been followed by a reasonably productive meeting with Sydnay. Sydnay had been more hostile to the 2+2 concept because of the disastrous first attempt that had left her smarting. But Pauline had assuaged Sydnay's feelings of hostility through her positive approach and problem-solving demeanor. The meeting had finished on an upbeat note with Sydnay agreeing to get her orders into the production department's system in a timelier manner. She had not realized that the department operated with a two-day planning horizon and that her urgent requests for same-day production and delivery caused chaos throughout the production division.

> A 2+2 success: everyone looks forward to feedback.

Sydnay was also clearly surprised that Pauline had noticed that her number of new customers had increased for the fourth time in that many months. She said that she had no idea Pauline was aware of her efforts to bring in new customers. Pauline had been prepared with one other compliment and one other suggestion, but the meeting had gone so well with the first two issues that she wisely decided the others could be deferred until the next meeting.

Pauline began to look forward to the 2+2 meetings with all her other people. *Amazing,* she thought. *I've never looked forward to a feedback meeting before!*

KEY TAKEAWAYS

- A 2+2 conversation provides structure for meaningful communication and problem solving.

- It need not be explicitly coupled with the formal performance appraisal system.

- Encouraging people to speak and then listening carefully to their comments is a critical part of the feedback process.

TWELVE

The Integrated Follow-Up

Within just three weeks, Pauline had completed her first round of 2+2 conversations and was still excited about the approach. She was convinced that this was indeed a great way to provide regular, constructive feedback to her staff. She felt that she was successfully eliminating the need for her people to be mind readers. Instead she was focusing their efforts on becoming more effective sales personnel.

Although she was basically pleased with her experience with 2+2 thus far, she was concerned that several of the discussions had not gone as smoothly as she had hoped. The disappointing sessions had generally involved the lower-performing people with whom she had experienced numerous run-ins in the past. She attributed the difficulty with those 2+2 encounters to the fact that her previous personal communication style had been extremely passive and unsystematic—unless a really big problem had emerged. Because of this old style, several of the people with whom she had regularly discussed problems had become habitually defensive. It would take time, she decided, to gain their confidence in her new approach.

As she reflected further on her first round of discussions, she concluded that she still needed to fine-tune her 2+2 skills. She set a goal for herself—that of having 2+2 institutionalized as a regular practice in her department by the end of the next quarter. She would first strive to perfect 2+2 as a vehicle for feedback to her people. She hoped that this would set an example that could be extended to peer-provided 2+2. Ultimately, she wanted to solicit 2+2 feedback from customers. *What a wonderful opportunity to send a signal to our customers that we want to improve our performance*, she thought.

+ + +

As Pauline made the rounds during the next few weeks to conduct her second set of 2+2 sessions, she was surprised to find that people's levels of improvement varied tremendously. Percy and Sydnay had both immediately acted on the earlier conversations and had made substantial progress.

Percy had called on a number of the heavy industry accounts and had made several sales to customers who had not purchased from the company in some time.

Sydnay had likewise worked hard to make improvements in the timely submission of her orders. In fact, she had e-mailed Pauline with the news that her credibility with the production department had strengthened so dramatically that she had been able to get the department to complete two rush orders that had come in unexpectedly from a longtime customer. Percy and Sydnay both expressed the belief that the 2+2 conversations had helped them do their jobs more effectively. Others in Pauline's department seemed to have benefited from the conversations as well.

However, when Pauline met for the second time with her two problem people, she discovered that they had not made any changes. Both had given their verbal agreement to a plan for improvement, but they had not taken any concrete steps to better their performance. Pauline had no choice but to raise the same two issues again. She received the same response. "I'll improve," they both promised. How could she hold these people accountable? The very informality of the system made it non-threatening but also lacking in teeth. Could she find a way to maintain the informality yet ensure accountability?

Since Pauline hadn't talked to Audrey for some time, she decided to give her mentor a call, bring her up to date on her progress, and ask for her advice on how to move the program forward.

Pauline was pleased that Audrey was in her office and readily agreed to meet for lunch the following week. Pauline immediately began to prepare questions for the meeting.

At the appointed time, Pauline met Audrey at The Italian Café. Audrey briefly shared everything that had been happening at the company—Percy's return and her recent successes with 2+2.

"I'm happy to hear that, overall, things have gone so well!" Audrey said in response to Pauline's informal report. "You've done a great job getting 2+2 up and running in such a short period of time. I really like the way that you are preparing for each of your meetings. Homework is the foundation for good feedback."

"Thanks, Audrey," Pauline interjected. "The 2+2 program is helping in so many ways."

"It sounds to me that you're ready to use one more secret of 2+2: follow-up. This is an extremely important part of mastering the feedback process. Too many managers offer great ideas and suggestions to their people without any follow-up. In many cases, managers don't notice whether their people have acted upon the 2+2 conversations. Worse yet, they send the signal to their people that they don't care! Follow-up is an important way to get the most impact out of your 2+2 conversations."

> Follow-up says you care.

Audrey suggested that there were a couple of areas where Pauline could focus her attention as she began to put the secret of follow-up to work.

"Be prepared to schedule a follow-up meeting or phone call after any of your 2+2 discussions. You'll have to determine when a meeting might be the most effective—or when a phone call might suffice. Often, additional meetings and calls are unnecessary and not helpful for either manager or employee. But sometimes a follow-up meeting or a phone call can make all the difference. Follow-up is just one more opportunity to remain aware of and guide a person's progress. Either you'll be able to reinforce what has been accomplished following a 2+2 session or you'll have an opportunity to take further action as necessary to ensure that your people are responding appropriately to 2+2 feedback."

"That makes a lot of sense," said Pauline. "I've been really perplexed by the way that some people—usually my more marginal performers—come across as agreeable during my conversations with them, but nothing seems to change after we've met."

"A follow-up meeting doesn't guarantee compliance," Audrey admitted, "but it certainly offers you a systematic way to monitor the progress of any given employee and take further action as needed. And, of course, sometimes more than one follow-up session is necessary.

"Remember, Pauline, a sense of accountability is crucial if your feedback is to be effective."

"I understand that accountability is important," Pauline responded. "I'm just concerned that it will get in the way of the helpful and positive tone of my 2+2 meetings. If I keep checking up on my people, they will feel that I don't trust them."

Follow-up builds accountability.

"I think you are making too much of a contradiction out of *helpfulness* and *accountability*," Audrey said. "I find that managing for high performance requires comfort with seemingly paradoxical requirements. As a manager, one of your most important roles is to emphasize and model helpfulness and accountability. That's why the secret of follow-up is so important. For instance, what would you think if I called you tomorrow and asked how things were going? Would you be offended?"

"Of course not. I'd take it as a compliment that you were concerned enough to take the time to give me a call."

"You see what I mean? Why wouldn't your people have the same response to you as you follow up to see how things are going and also take the time to work with them further if necessary? And in the many instances where you discover that things are going well, you have a wonderful opportunity to compliment those people on their improvement. Soon after, your people will come to expect follow-up and prepare themselves for the accountability it encourages.

"If your feedback is reasonable and actionable, you have every reason to expect action will be taken. If a handful of people are not doing anything to improve, you may need to take more drastic steps. Those few problem people need to know that their work is unacceptable so that they have a chance to improve—before you discipline them in some way."

"You're right again, Audrey. I'm beginning to understand how and why accountability and helpfulness fit together. In most cases, the follow-up will simply give me a chance to reinforce good work, but where my feedback hasn't been taken seriously, I can hopefully help my people get back on track before they get into more serious trouble."

"That's exactly it, Pauline."

As they paid the check and got up to leave, Audrey said, "Give me a call anytime. I'm happy to do anything I can to be of help. In fact, I think that what you're doing in your department could very well spread to other departments in your company—once they see the impact that you're having on productivity and profits!"

KEY TAKEAWAYS

- Follow-up is a critical means for reinforcing feedback.
- Follow-up can be conducted informally or formally depending upon the situation.
- Set follow-up to
  - Assess progress after an appropriate interval.
  - Determine if the agreed-upon course of action is working.
  - Hold people accountable for agreed-upon changes.
  - Reinforce improvement.
  - Outline further need for change.

THIRTEEN

Creating a Sustainable 2+2 Program

In the weeks that followed, Pauline committed to scheduling a follow-up to each 2+2 meeting. This would give her the chance to touch base quickly and verify that what had been discussed was being implemented.

When things were going smoothly, the follow-up phone calls could be short and would serve as a brief wrap-up until the next 2+2 session. If satisfactory improvement had not been made, she would take further action. This could take several forms. When the person appeared to have made a good will effort, the initial approach might simply be more problem solving and action planning with another follow-up date set.

In rarer cases—where the problem appeared to be a lack of sufficient follow-through on the part of one of her people—Pauline could take one of several approaches. She could, for example, schedule an earlier-than-typical follow-up meeting to monitor the person's progress more closely. When it seemed appropriate, she could even warn the person, either informally or formally, that if his or her performance did not improve, the result could be disciplinary action.

Pauline liked the fact that when people had made progress, she had the opportunity to recognize their accomplishments and reinforce the direction in which they were headed. When insufficient or no progress had been made, she could uncover this fact quickly and take steps to change the situation. She had a variety of new approaches to try with 2+2.

At first she was tempted to set a routine two-week follow-up date. This would be long enough to allow for progress and yet short enough to give additional feedback to people who needed it quickly. But as she thought about it further, she realized that she would prefer to set different follow-up times for different people and different circumstances. For example, when employee safety or the company's reputation was at stake, immediate follow-up would be warranted. In other cases—particularly with her stronger, more independent people—follow-up might not be necessary for several weeks. Of course, she would continue to interact with her people on a routine basis. That would provide additional opportunities for less-structured discussions.

By the end of the third round, Pauline felt she had a good system in place. The backbone consisted of an initial monthly 2+2 meeting with follow-up, as necessary, set for a time consistent with the needs of each individual.

Pauline was amazed by how little extra time the 2+2 process took. Much of her "homework" could be done on the fly. When she noted something that needed to be covered in a 2+2 session, she would make a brief note to herself and continue with what she was doing. This did not replace the need for a few minutes of systematic preparation for each meeting, but it made the process much more manageable.

She also discovered that the meetings themselves took almost no extra time. She found that instead of scheduling a series of specific 2+2s at the beginning of each monthly cycle, in most cases, she could hold 2+2 conversations without making additional visits to people's offices. Of course, when it made sense to do so, she could still make a separate visit. Her follow-ups were also very time efficient, often combined with other meetings. Many even took place over the phone.

By the fourth round, Pauline found that even some of her problem people were taking quick action on 2+2 suggestions. She assumed that was because they knew a follow-up would take place, so they had a greater incentive to make some acceptable progress. Pauline was convinced that the follow-up—either by phone or in person—was a very powerful part of an effective 2+2 system.

✚ ✚ ✚

One day Percy dropped by Pauline's office unexpectedly. "Do you have a few minutes?"

"Sure, Percy, what's on your mind?"

"Pauline, I've been really impressed with the way you've used 2+2 with us. It has helped me know where I stand on a number of important issues. Working together, we've solved several important problems that could have festered indefinitely if you hadn't raised them with me. It has also made me really happy to know you appreciate some of the successes I've had. Thanks to the changes you've made, this company is becoming a great place to work. I'm glad you hired me back!"

> Great feedback produces a great job. A great job produces a great workplace.

KEY TAKEAWAYS

- Follow-up encourages even reticent employees to improve.

- Formula 2+2 does not require a great deal of time.

- A rhythm of feedback can be developed where 2+2 becomes a regular and appreciated part of the workplace experience.

- Formula 2+2 helps employees do a great job and contributes to organizational success!

FOURTEEN

Epilogue
Two Years Later

Tommy Titan was out of control and Percy Pershing knew what might help. That's because he had just been transferred to Tommy's department as sales manager. Percy had inherited an organization that appeared to be desperately in need of some midcourse corrections.

Tomorrow, Percy decided, he would hold his first staff meeting and introduce the 2+2 system of performance feedback to his team. He expected that he could have the full 2+2 system in place by the end of the year—if, that is, he gained the necessary credibility with his people.

Meanwhile, he was looking forward to having lunch later that day with his mentor, Pauline. Even though he had been an early participant in the 2+2 system in Pauline's department, he had many questions on which he wanted to get her advice before he launched the system on his own.

At precisely 11:30, Pauline knocked on Percy's office door. Percy hit a final key on his computer to send a broadcast message to his staff and greeted Pauline warmly.

"Great to see you," he said. "How about trying the new deli bar in the cafeteria?"

"Okay by me," Pauline replied, and they were on their way down three flights of stairs to the cafeteria commons.

As they munched on their subs, they reminisced about the early days of the 2+2 system and how their organization had won the outstanding departmental improvement award the following year. Amazingly, more than half of the company was using 2+2 at this point—mostly the direct result of Pauline's success.

> The power of 2+2: everyone wins—and knows it!

"You know," said Percy, "more than anything, I was surprised at the fact that even though it took many of our colleagues some time to get used to the idea, virtually everyone in the department really takes 2+2 seriously. With 2+2, everyone wins—and knows it!"

Pauline was pleased to hear this. "Candidly, I can tell you that one of the reasons I recommended you for this promotion was the fact that so many of your associates not only valued your peer feedback but really began to look toward you as a mentor and confidant. If there is anyone qualified to turn your new department around, it is definitely you."

"Thanks for the compliment, Pauline. I'm really looking forward to working with my new staff to see what we can do together to take this department to the top. Certainly 2+2 will be a solid part of my strategy to give intensive, constructive feedback to my people. As important as that is on an ongoing basis, it is going to be particularly crucial as we engage in some substantial departmental transformation.

"You know," Percy continued, "I've been thinking. This 2+2 stuff is so powerful that it could well be applied in other settings. Perhaps parents could use it as a way to improve communication within their families. And think about teachers. Imagine how much 2+2 could help teachers improve education if they occasionally visited other classrooms and provided some feedback to each other. At the same time, they could develop a 2+2 approach for their students. Imagine how kids would respond to teachers who not only focused on their weaknesses but systematically praised their strengths!"

"You're right, Percy," Pauline said with a wink, "but those are topics for other books."

2+2

Authors' Final Note

Midcourse corrections have been a major feature in the development of many recent technologies. Technical midcourse correction capabilities make it possible for computers to learn from their mistakes and improve their power and performance over time. Autopilots on aircraft use midcourse corrections to bring planes in for safe landings in zero-visibility conditions. And, of course, the Mars Rovers represent the most distant land vehicles ever to receive midcourse corrections from humans as they have rolled sedately across the Mars landscape—millions of miles from Earth.

While we have perfected our *technical* midcourse correction capabilities beyond our wildest dreams of even ten years ago, most managers are still frustrated by their inability to achieve effective *human* midcourse corrections within their organizations.

Whether they work in the same room as their managers or perhaps halfway around the world across cultures and time zones, most managers and their employees want to work more effectively with each other. They want to share and receive feedback that will help correct areas in need of improvement and will also recognize and reinforce the many successes. The 2+2 process of continuous and focused feedback can bring a team closer together in a spirit of collaboration.

As Pauline discovered, no feedback system can be implemented overnight. The successful launch of any new organizational system requires patience and wisdom. But the real question is, Where do you start? The beauty of 2+2 is that you can start anywhere—from simply combining 2+2 compliments and suggestions into a short conversation with an employee to initiating a more structured program. The 2+2 system is easy to implement and easy to modify over time.

We invite you to try the 2+2 system. We believe that this simple but powerful concept will assist you in your efforts to give and receive effective feedback—wherever you find yourself in the organization. Formula 2+2 can help you make your organization more pleasant, more dynamic, and more productive.

Give it a try!

THE SECRETS OF 2+2

Formula 2+2: Two compliments and two suggestions!

BALANCE

TIMELINESS

FOCUS

SPECIFICITY

FOLLOW-UP

- *Balance* compliments and suggestions for improvement.
- Provide feedback in a *timely* fashion.
- *Focus* feedback on the highest priority areas.
- Support feedback with *specific* examples.
- Reinforce feedback with appropriate *follow-up*.

PAULINE'S 2+2 PREPARATION CHECKLIST

❏ Provide feedback as close to the incident as possible.

❏ Prepare at least one compliment and one suggested improvement.

❏ Identify the highest-priority issues.

❏ Use specific examples to reinforce each point.

❏ Schedule 2+2 sessions in advance until your staff feel comfortable with spontaneous sessions.

❏ Schedule a follow-up session to discuss progress.

Feedback: Always delivered in the Spirit of 2+2!

JOY

HELPFULNESS

ENCOURAGEMENT

SINCERE CONCERN FOR PEOPLE

CELEBRATE SUCCESS!

ACKNOWLEDGMENTS

The writing and editing of *Formula* 2+2 involved the help of many people to whom we are truly indebted. While it is never possible to mention all contributors by name, we want to acknowledge a number of special and dear family members and friends who generously offered their love, time, and support to this project.

We thank Doug's wife and daughters (Dwight's daughter-in-law and granddaughters), Ginny, Lindsay, and Sydnay, for unwavering love, patience, and support during a lengthy writing process. They helped brainstorm names used in the book and reviewed some of the early manuscripts. Ginny's emphasis on the importance of respecting employee dignity was especially helpful.

We are equally grateful to Dwight's wife (Doug's mother), Carole, for her great help in reviewing numerous iterations of the manuscript and for providing continuing feedback and midcourse corrections as the book developed. Her keen editorial eye picked out many grammatical transgressions and more importantly identified several key opportunities for improving the structure and flow of the story.

Ken Blanchard is a dear friend and served as an ongoing source of encouragement throughout the project. Whether finding time in his busy schedule for a quick conference call or stopping off at a Denver Denny's restaurant to meet at 11 p.m. enroute from the airport to Aspen, he generously shared his time and ideas with us as the book developed and progressed from concept to completion. We also offer a special word of thanks to the Blanchard staff—most particularly Dottie Hamilt and Martha Lawrence, who helped keep us in touch with Ken and provided great logistical support as we passed manuscripts and ideas back and forth.

Steve Gottry provided great help in the editorial phase of the development of this book. Steve has a real knack for fine-tuning a story line and providing a bright polish to prose.

The Berrett-Koehler staff were wonderful to work with. Their support resulted in a much-improved product. Special thanks to Steve Piersanti and Jeevan Sivasubramaniam for their wisdom and guidance along the way.

We would also like to extend thanks to the High Performance Management MBA core course faculty team at the University of Denver. Their adoption of the 2+2 approach as a peer feedback mechanism for student teams was not only a great show of confidence in the concept but also provided a rich forum for collegial discussion about the implementation of 2+2. We extend special thanks to faculty team members R. J. Graham and Cindi Fukami for their thoughtful review of early manuscripts. Cindi's metaphor of performance appraisal as "a trip to the dentist" helped shape a key concept in our book.

At Old Dominion University, Bob Brinton, now community superintendent of schools for the Department of Defense Schools in Camp Lejeune, North Carolina, and Alyce LeBlanc (coauthor of sister publication *Collaborative Peer Coaching That Improves Instruction: The 2+2 Performance Appraisal Model*, published by Corwin Press), Patrick O'Shea, Simon Richmond, Jennifer Kemp, Lee Vartanian, Jonathan Higgens, Rus Higley, Steve Corson, and Dale Baird contributed to the shaping and reshaping of the ideas and ideals of 2+2.

We are also grateful to The Ministry of Education in Namibia, UNESCO, and Chief Technical Advisor Peter Higgs for providing the original venue for the development of 2+2 in rural schools in Namibia. What started as a modest concept to help teachers build opportunities for continuous improvement into remote school settings through systematic and helpful peer feedback has grown into a system that has been implemented in business, public sector, and not-for-profit organizations on four continents. We think it particularly appropriate that an approach emerging out of rural African villages has demonstrated the potential for transforming the effectiveness of businesses throughout the world. This is what a global learning community is truly all about.

Our enthusiasm for the spirit of 2+2 is inspired by the teachings of the Bahá'í faith. These teachings embrace consultation, encouragement, and *feedback* and emphasize the importance of unity for the success of any endeavor.

Finally, this project would not have been completed without the help of many people too numerous to mention in a short section called "Acknowledgments." Many people have read earlier versions of our manuscript and provided extremely useful feedback—often in the form of 2+2 conversations, e-mails, or phone calls. To all of these individuals, we offer our heartiest thanks and deepest gratitude.

ABOUT THE AUTHORS

Douglas B. Allen is associate professor of management at the University of Denver Daniels College of Business. He is also a guest professor at Renmin (People's) University Business School in Beijing, China, and a visiting professor at Tongji University in Shanghai, China. He received his doctorate from the University of Michigan, a masters of business administration from Harvard, and a bachelor of science degree from the University of Zimbabwe.

Previously, Doug worked as a human resource management specialist at Chrysler World Headquarters and as an international placement consultant at the Bahá'í National Center. He has consulted with and conducted training programs for many organizations, including Amoco, Boeing, Chrysler, General Electric, Honeywell, Nokia (China), and Tata (India).

Doug has published articles and makes frequent presentations on management in China, globalization, human resource management, and cross-cultural and diversity issues, as well as the 2+2 feedback system to a wide variety of conferences and organizations. He has made thirty visits to China and has lived, traveled, and/or worked in over forty-five other countries in Africa, Asia, Europe, and the Americas.

Dwight W. Allen is Eminent Scholar of Educational Reform at Old Dominion University and has developed educational reform initiatives for more than forty years. At Stanford University he was director of teacher education and helped develop an award-winning internship program. As dean of education at the University of Massachusetts he helped develop over twenty simultaneous teacher training programs to explore the relative efficacy of a variety of theoretical models, one winning an award as the outstanding program of the year from the American Association of Colleges of Teacher Education. At Old Dominion University he cofounded the PRIME program in Norfolk Public Schools involving many systemic change initiatives focused on teacher empowerment. He has served as a consultant to more than one hundred national, state, and local school authorities.

Dwight has worked with UNESCO, where he was founding chief technical advisor for the first National Teacher Training College in Lesotho and was technical advisor for in-service teacher training programs in Malawi and Namibia. It was in Namibia that the idea for 2+2 was first developed. For the past eleven years, he has served with the United Nations Development Program as chief technical advisor and international advisor for the largest UNDP education programs in China.

Dwight is the author of nine books on educational reform and teacher education, the latest of which is *American Schools: The 100 Billion Dollar Challenge* (with Bill Cosby). He has visited China over twenty times and has lived, worked, and/or traveled in over sixty countries in Africa, Asia, Europe, and the Americas.

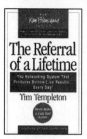

The Referral of a Lifetime
The Networking System That Produces Bottom-Line Results... Every Day!

Tim Templeton

Part of The Ken Blanchard Series, *The Referral of a Lifetime* teaches a step-by-step system that will allow anyone to generate a steady stream of new business through consistent referrals from existing customers and friends and, at the same time, maximize business with existing customers.

Hardcover • ISBN 1-57675-240-2 • Item #52402 $19.95

The Serving Leader
5 Powerful Actions That Will Transform Your Team, Your Business, and Your Community

Ken Jennings and John Stahl-Wert

At a time of increasing concern about ethics at the top, *The Serving Leader* makes the case for an approach to leadership that is both more moral and more effective than the ruthless, anything-for-the-bottom-line approach that has brought disgrace to many once-mighty organizations. This is the most practical guide available to implementing servant leadership.

Hardcover • ISBN 1-57675-265-8 • Item #52658 $19.95

Paperback • ISBN 1-57675-308-5 • Item #53085 $14.95

Your Leadership Legacy
The Difference You Make in People's Lives

Marta Brooks, Julie Stark, and Sarah Caverhill

Your leadership legacy is the sum total of the difference you make in people's lives, directly and indirectly, formally and informally. The challenge is how to live in a way that creates a legacy that will make a positive difference in the lives of those around you. *Your Leadership Legacy* shows you how to live a meaningful legacy.

Hardcover • ISBN 1-57675-287-9 • Item #52879 $19.95

Berrett-Koehler Publishers
PO Box 565, Williston, VT 05495-9900
Call toll-free! **800-929-2929** 7 am-9 pm EST

Or fax your order to 1-802-864-7626
For fastest service order online: **www.bkconnection.com**

AMERICAN SCHOOLS
The $100 Billion Dollar Challenge

Dwight Allen, Ed.D. and
William H. Cosby, Jr., Ed.D.

From Bill Cosby, actor, entertainer, and *New York Times* bestselling author of *Fatherhood and Congratulations (Now What?)* comes a groundbreaking book with the potential to reinvent education in America.

Exchanging comedy for community activism, Bill Cosby teams up with Dwight Allen, Eminent Professor of Education Reform at Old Dominion University, to issue a challenge to the federal government and the new captains of industry: produce one hundred billion dollars and reform, revamp, and reinvent our schools.

Together, Cosby and Allen do more than discuss the problems—the crumbling buildings, flagging test scores, and failing students—they offer concrete solutions, outlining a point-by-point plan for putting dot-com dollars to work.

Available wherever e-books are sold. Or, to order a Print-on-Demand copy (ISBN: 075955000X), please call Time Warner Book Group Customer Service 1-800-759-0190.

Collaborative Peer Coaching That Improves Instruction
The 2+2 Performance Appraisal Model

Dwight W. Allen and Alyce C. Le Blanc

Dramatically enhance teaching and learning by reviving teacher collaboration!

The 2+2 method, a practice where teachers visit each other's classrooms and provide two compliments and two suggestions for improvement, not only enhances teaching skills and student learning, but also increases job satisfaction. Discover how 2+2 restores the vital connections between teachers and students, teachers and administrators, and teachers and teachers • Encourages teaching and learning to develop beyond what standardized tests reveal • Provides a low-cost, easy-to-implement program that is realistic, given teacher time constraints and limited school budgets.

Transforms schools into cultures of collaborative teaching and learning

Available October 2004 • www.corwinpress.com